First published 2021

(c) 2021 Dominic Salles

All rights reserved. The right of Dominic Salles to be identified as the   of this work has been asserted by them in accordance with the Copyright, Designs and Patents Act 1988. No part of this work may be reproduced, stored in a retrieval system, transmitted in any form or by any means, electronical, mechanical, photocopying, recording, or otherwise, without the prior permission of the Author.

Dominic Salles still lives in Swindon, with his workaholic wife Deirdre. His jiu-jitsu-loving ex-engineer son, Harry, has moved to Shoreditch and lives on the site of Shakespeare's first theatre. Destiny.

His daughter Jess is educating students in Wales because, now Brexit is done, Brussels isn't stepping in to help the Welsh any more. She is learning to surf. Destiny rides again – I am going snowboarding for three months in January 2022, surfing the snow. I have paid! His sister Jacey is famous for her Spanish accent, on your TV screens, and is also filming in Wales. Casualty, in case you are interested. She would be hilarious in her own YouTube channel.

His 2006 Prius has just died and been rein*car*nated (who writes these puns?) as a 2019 Prius. Bob is no more. He is never getting another dog.

His YouTube channel, Mr Salles Teaches English, will one day earn him a living – perhaps when exams return. Your cloud is his silver lining.

Contents Page

Introduction	3
Choosing the Right VERBS	5
Choosing Appropriate Vocabulary ADJECTIVES	7
Choosing Appropriate Vocabulary ADVERBS	10
Using CONTRAST	12
Using Imagery SIMILE	17
Using Imagery METAPHOR	20
Using Imagery EXTENDED METAPHOR	26
Using the Senses	31
What Dickens Teaches Us About Smell	34
What Dickens Teaches Us About Sound	36
Creating a Soundscape	40
What Dickens Teaches Us About Harsh Sounds	43
What Dickens Teaches Us About Soft Sounds	44
Journeys Through Memory	46
Journeys Through a Place You Know Well	49
Journey Through the Park	49
Journey Through the House as Memories	51
Seafront Journey - putting it all together	54
Journey Through Violent Memories	58
Journey Through a Beach	61
A Journey Through the Seasons	65
Journeys Through the Eyes of a Persona	67
Journey Through Close Up	67
Journey: Dog's Eye View	74
A Grandfather's Journey Round the Home	76
Journey Through an Image	78
Journey Through a Painting in an Art Gallery	78
Journey Through a Photograph in an Art Gallery	81
Answer Based on the AQA Paper 1 from June 2019	83
Journey Through Metaphor	86
A Student's Journey Taking an Exam	86
A Toddler's Journey Through Space	87
Just Show me Methods for the Exam!	88
Weather Personification	88
The Kingsdown Method Checklist	90
Kingsdown Exam Method – Model Answer	91
Kingsdown Method 2	92
Six Cameras Method	94
So what do you know?	97
Yasmine's Work	98

Introduction to the Mr Salles Ultimate Guide to Description

Ok, why would you buy this instead of the Quick Guide to Awesome Description? That's easy. I want to teach you how to write. Really write, so that your writing would fit into real books.

The descriptions you are asked to write at GCSE are mostly unhelpful. Real writers don't write the way we teach descriptions in school.

But what if I could help you learn to write brilliantly, AND get top grades at school? Well, I really can. This guide will do it for you.

You can follow it as a course, or you can simply read the 20+ grade 9 descriptions. That's right, over 20 top grade descriptions! I know, I should be selling this guide for £12.99 – the value is unbelievable.

Still not sure you want to put in the effort? No problem. I've got you covered. At the end you'll find a section on exam methods, just to get you through the exam as quickly as possible.

My Story

I've been an English teacher for 28 years. My YouTube channel, Mr Salles Teaches English, and my revision guides teach anyone how to get top grades. I've written the top selling guides on description and GCSE story writing on Amazon. 27% of my viewers say that my videos helped them improve by at least 3 GCSE grades.

Descriptive writing is hard. You need to write between 350-500 words and remember a dozen techniques, and then write something you would almost never actually see in a novel. Because people won't read novels which are full of long descriptions!

The Secrets to Great Descriptive Writing

1. Finding out what great writers do, and how they do it.

2. Finding out what you are getting wrong, and how to fix it.

3. Reading lots of grade 9 complete descriptions (at least 20 in this guide).

4. Practise writing your own.

   The Challenges of Learning to Write Description

   - There are too many descriptive techniques.
   - The exam questions are uninspiring.
   - Novelists don't write 350 - 500 word descriptions.
   - Teachers don't give you 10 top grade descriptions to learn from, never mind 20!

Guide Contents

1. **Verbs:** The most powerful words you'll ever use are verbs. That's right, not fancy, Thesaurus-like vocabulary, but carefully chosen verbs. Get these right, and you'll instantly improve.

2. **Vocabulary:** Learn how to choose vocabulary which helps your writing come alive, rather than create an over the top mess. Why adverbs are rarely a good idea.

3. **Contrast:** Understand how contrast is the hidden skill of all good description. The secret sauce.

4. **Similes:** How to use similes and why they so often go wrong.

5. **Metaphors:** How metaphors are twice as powerful as similes and how to develop personification and extended metaphors.

6. **The Senses:** Why description using the senses so often goes wrong, and how real writers get it right.

7. **A Soundscape:** How to create a soundscape, so that your writing sounds amazing out loud. Learn how to control harsh and soft sounds, and why alliteration often gets in the way.

8. **How to Structure Your Description:** as a journey, so that it is always interesting.

9. **Read 20 Model Answers:** Grade 9 descriptions, so you gain complete understanding of how to describe for top grades.

10. **How to create a persona**, so your descriptions are twice as effective.

11. **How to treat the picture as a work of art** in an art gallery.

12. **Just Show Me How to Pass:** 4 powerful methods of approaching the exam.

13. **Examples of student writing**, showing you how to move from grade 7 to grade 9.

    What Else?

    - At least 20 top grade descriptions which you can adapt, learn from and imitate. Don't copy them and risk plagiarism!

    - You will know how to tackle any description question, and any image.

    - You will be able to adapt any description to a story (in case you have to write a story in the exam).

    - You'll have everything you need for revision, right up to the exam.

    - You'll be able to correct any weakness your teacher spots, by going back to the relevant section of the course to re-teach you.

    - You'll be a good writer, not just for the exam, but for life.

Choosing the Right Verbs

What is a Verb?

It is not just a 'doing word'. We also have states, shown by the verb **to be**. The verb to be is unusual. We say, *I am, she is, he was, they will, we were*, not *we be, I be, he be, they bill, we beed*.

Verb: a word used to describe an action, state of being, or occurrence.

Test on Verbs

Identify the verbs in each of the following:

1. The elephant exploded with hysterical laughter.
2. The troop of gorillas beat their chests violently at the wicked hunters.
3. The teacher was delightfully surprised by the student's behaviour.

Answers: exploded, beat, surprised.

Task: identify the eight verbs

I opened the door, walked through the hall, and entered the kitchen. Here, I cooked a curry with a wok and then served it up on the plate. I ate quickly, before sitting down in front of the television to watch my favourite reality show.

Choose better verbs to focus on sound and more interesting action (see my version below)

*I **clattered** through the door, **skidded** through the hall and **slid** into the kitchen. Here, my curry **sizzled** in the wok, and I **dolloped** it on a plate. I **gulped** it down, before **crashing** in front of the television to **wallow** in my favourite reality show.*

Notice how these verbs recreate sounds. Good writers don't slow their writing down by telling us what sounds could be heard. Much of this work is done through verb choice, and you can see that **clattered, skidded, sizzled, gulped,** and **crashing** all suggest a variety of sounds to go with their actions.

The second thing to notice about all these verbs is how they work as descriptions of the character. They are all linked to give a very clear picture of someone who is in a rush, very hungry, and who gives in to all their appetites.

Your Turn: Can you spot the verbs?

The surfer moved slowly and silently across the waves, out to sea. She looked behind her, trying to time the next big wave. Now she paddled hard, pushing with her palms, ready to surf the wave.

Just in time, she straightened her arms, sat up, and then got to her feet. The board was steady beneath her and she prepared for the coming rush. As the wave got bigger, she rode on its crest. Her board got quicker as she turned it from side to side, keen to stay on the surface as long as she could. She bent her knees to cope with the force of the wave and rode it towards the beach.

Answers: Verbs are in bold.

The surfer **moved** slowly and silently across the waves, out to sea. She **looked** behind her, **trying to time** the next big wave. Now she **paddled** hard, **pushing** with her palms, ready **to surf** the wave.

Just in time, she **straightened** her arms, **sat up**, and then **got to** her feet. The board **was** steady beneath her and she **prepared** for the coming rush. As the wave **got bigger**, she **rode** on its crest. Her board **got quicker** as she **turned it** from side to side, keen **to stay** on the surface as long as she **could**. She **bent** her knees **to cope** with the force of the wave and **rode it** towards the beach.

Did you spot the state - 'the board was steady'?

How to make verbs more powerful

Read this paragraph and change many of the verbs to make it more informative.

The dog ran on, as she cycled behind him, calling for him to come back. Fenton kept on going, getting further away, as she pedalled as fast as she could. She could hear his excited barks as he called out to other dogs. She could tell where he was from the flocks of birds rising from the long grass and trees. She wondered why she hadn't put him on a lead when they set off.

This is how my verb choice changed the paragraph:
The dog **leapt** ahead, as she **cycled** behind him, **yelling** for him to come back. Fenton **ignored** her, **sprinting** further away, as she **pumped** the pedals as hard as she could. His excited barks **alarmed** her as he **tormented** other dogs. She **tracked** him to where flocks of birds **burst** from the long grass and trees. She **reprimanded** herself for not **tying** him on a lead when they set off.

Once again, notice how these verbs give us a real description of the character of this dog. Fenton is deliberately misbehaving and excited. Similarly, we understand the character of his owner who is starting to panic. So you can see that verbs don't just tell you what the action is, they describe the character's personality and their feelings. This is why verbs are the building blocks of all good writing.

Choosing Appropriate Vocabulary

Adjectives

An adjective describes a noun or a pronoun. Let's see what you know.

Which of these is **never** an adjective?
- red
- table
- flat
- ridiculous

Which of these is **never** an adjective?
- rose
- violent
- violet
- violin

Which of these is **never** an adjective?
- wonderful
- wonder
- wishful
- withering

Which word is the **adjective** in this sentence? *The cat's claws painfully sprang from its enormous paws.*
- enormous
- claws
- painfully
- paws

Which word is the **adjective** in this sentence? *My sister's dress is bigger than my brother's tent for camping happily in the garden.*
- brother's
- sister's
- bigger
- garden
- happily

Spot the Adjectives

Darkness encapsulated the only source of light shining from the station, as the immensely sinister train glided in my path, creating a distasteful and uneasy feeling in the air. Charred as black as the soul of a devil, the dilapidated doors drearily opened. I felt a stab of cold pierce through my weary heart and numbness ran through my body.

Answers

Darkness encapsulated the only source of light shining from the station, as the immensely sinister train glided in my path, creating a distasteful and uneasy feeling in the air. Charred as black as the soul of a devil, the dilapidated doors drearily opened. I felt a stab of cold pierce through my weary heart and numbness ran through my body.

Less is More

- When students have learned lots of descriptive techniques, their writing often gets worse.
- This is natural. It is a state where we are moving from novice to expert.
- What gets worse? The writing is so packed with descriptive techniques that it stops being easy to read, like the paragraph above.

Your Task

1. Rewrite it so that it is no more than 40 words long.
2. It must have the same mood and meaning.
3. But get rid of lots of description which isn't needed.

Show, Don't Tell

When I rewrite this, I try to get rid of anything the reader can work out for themselves. So from my version below, the reader can work out that it is dark, and the atmosphere is sinister. I don't have to tell them.

Mr Salles' Rewrite (34 Words)

A single light stared out from the station. I was alone on the platform. The train glided, silent in the still, cold air and stopped. I reached for the door with a numb heart.

Task

- Note down 3 things you have learned to improve your writing.
- Notice that there are problems with too much alliteration, as you saw with the dreary dilapidated doors.
- Notice that sibilance can be used repeatedly to create the right atmosphere – but I have still separated **single, stared, station** with other words so that they are not listed together. I've done the **same with silent, still**, stopped.

1. _____
2. _____
3. _____

Your Turn: Redraft the following paragraph using SHOW DON'T TELL.

- **Concentrate on changing verbs and adjectives – but change as much as you want.**
- **You must keep the same atmosphere and events.**

- **Like the writing of many students, this swaps between the present and past tenses. Write it in just the past tense.**

Lifelessly the driver who bears an empty expression upon his ghost like face stared at me with his queerly beady eyes and I felt a stinging sensation rip my insides; my senses urged me that something was not right; I decided to leave but grievously a skeletal hand grabbed my arm twisted it and flung me to the passenger seats. Glancing around cautiously, I made my way to an empty seat which was repugnant and was surrounded by aberrant passengers; who looked like prisoners with their uniform facial expression. Building up the courage and swallowing the fear, which was raging inside me, I solemnly whispered hello. Robotically each passenger blankly gazed at me, upon their foreheads were strange markings.
(119 words)

This is what it looks like when focusing on better verbs and adjectives to 'show not tell':
The driver stared through me, as I hesitated. He locked a **skeletal** hand on my wrist and jerked me inside. The passengers looked up as one, with the same **blank** eyes. I forced out a hello as I made my way to the **single empty** seat. As one, they lifted their gaze to me, which is when I noticed the markings.
(61 words)

Notice how the same sense of fear and alarm and strangeness is conveyed with far fewer words by focusing on the changes in adjective. This is a version of show don't tell. All writers want to convey the maximum mood and information with the fewest number of words.

You will also notice but I have got rid of all the adverbs. Adverbs tend to slow your writing down. Often this happens when you are actually trying to speed the pace up. For example, in this piece the writer wants to create a sense of danger and tension. We need fast paced events leading us towards some danger. However, the writer keeps adding sinister events, but then reduces their impact by over telling us what to think through the use of adverbs.

Look at my description to see how the reader can still work out the mood intended without the original adverbs: **lifelessly, grievously, cautiously, solemnly, robotically, blankly.**

Adverbs

The popular definition of an adverb is that it describes a verb. These words usually end in 'ly'. These are the kind of adverbs to avoid, as far as possible. Limit them in your writing.

There are also adverbs to show time, manner, place, or degree, which aren't really a problem to the pace of your writing, so feel free to keep them.

Let's look at how you can replace adverbs with verbs.

1. Goldilocks **ate greedily**, **devouring** *three* bowls of porridge.
2. Goldilocks **devoured** *all three* bowls of porridge.
3. Goldilocks **stuffed** herself with *three whole* bowls of porridge.

Notice that sentence one tells us how she ate, by using two verbs.

Sentence two improves things, showing us how she ate with just the one verb, devoured. The addition of "all" also **shows** us she is greedy, not just hungry. So we are **shown** how she is greedy, and we no longer need the adverb to **tell** us.

Sentence three gets rid of the confusion as to whether she is more hungry than greedy. Choosing the better verb "stuffed" **shows** us without doubt that she is greedy. This greed is now emphasised by swapping the adjective "all" with "whole". This **shows** us how she has eaten every last bit of full bowls of porridge, so we can be horrified at how greedy she really is.

Lesson 18 Why Adverbs are Dangerous!

1. So, you probably remember that adverbs get in the way of most writing, because they slow down time.
2. The right verb already tells you better than the wrong verb and an adverb. *She ran quickly* is not as informative as *she dashed, she sprinted, she hurried, she sped...*
3. However, if slowing down time is a superpower, we can choose a moment in time which we want to stretch out (endlessly!)
4. Below, I have fun with this idea - stretching out the agony of revising, then opening up an exam paper...

The Exam

The exam approached relentlessly, mercilessly. I revised haphazardly, sporadically, anxiously. Fortunately, after watching Mr Salles's videos regularly, religiously, reverently, I felt more prepared (probably). Confidently, creatively, I crafted perfect revision notes. Studying feverishly, ferociously, I felt fully prepared.

The exam arrived, and I entered the hall calmly, casually and commandingly. I blitzed the first four questions, quickly, cunningly, comprehensively.

Eventually, ecstatically, expectantly, I turned to the description question. It read: describe a moment when you felt unprepared: don't use adverbs.

I yelled out fiercely, fricatively, finally, something beginning with F.

- I hope this helps you remember that adverbs are useful for slowing down time – then have fun with them. But with everything else, just choose a better verb and adjective.

Adverbs Used to Slow Down Time in Normal Description

- Let's see what it looks like in normal writing, where you want to slow down time that builds tension.
- In the example below, Amal has suddenly come across an unexploded bomb while digging a pond in his garden.

How long ago was World War Two? Decades, thought Amal, searching **carefully** for any memory about defusing bombs. In films, they always cut wires **nervously**, sweat dripping **slowly** onto their shaking fingers.

The giant black, metal shape he had uncovered **unexpectedly** digging the garden, sat **menacingly**, but not quite **silently**. When he tapped it (oh so **gently**) Amal was sure he heard a steady tick.

Now each adverb shows us how much danger Amal is in. Although Amal is thinking **carefully**, this is also dangerous, as the bomb is ticking (which we are shown by the adverbial phrase 'not quite **silently**'). We expect an explosion is possible any second, because the bomb is sitting '**menacingly**'. But that moment is stretched out with the adverbial phrase 'oh so **gently**'. You get the idea. Slowing down time here really makes us invest in the character.

It is also a really easy way to stop your description becoming a story. The whole scene of reacting to the bomb might take only 10 minutes of real life – so it can't be a story. But it would be easy to draw it out over 500 words.

Using Contrast

Contrast is the secret sauce of great description. The problem with description is that it can be so boring. Nothing happens! Contrast forces things together in an uncomfortable way – so it always provides a sense of action – even when there are no actual events.

A great way to practise this is to introduce a 'but' into your description.

Contrast in BUT Sentences

A dozen cows **grazed** in the field, **but**

the earth was **parched** and the few ragged tufts of green didn't satisfy them.

Sunshine **blazed** upon the beach, **but**

the **freezing** sea left the bathers gasping for air.

Autumn **painted** the hills with browns, russets and golds, **but**

winter **washed** the scene with grey skies and snowy fields.

The girl sat **listening** to her friend's plans, **but**

she didn't dare **tell** him they were bound to fail.

1. Notice how a contrast is built around a near opposite.
2. Each contrast is made through choosing verbs.
3. Notice how it gives drama and tension to any description - it forces us to ask what might happen next.
4. Each sentence is built around 'But'

Practise this four yourself:

(Include a 'but' in the middle of each sentence to introduce the contrast).

1. Write one contrast about time or the seasons.
2. Write one contrast between character A and character B.
3. Write one contrast between air, earth, wind or fire.

Find the Contrast

- It comes from a real novel by a once famous writer. This is important, because everything you learn in this guide is to help you become a better writer, doing what real writers do.
- They have to make their descriptions work in a novel – whereas the descriptions students are forced to write in class are often unrealistic as they are packed with too many of the wrong descriptive techniques.
- Use two different colours to highlight the contrast in this extract.

Contrast can be built:

Around time:

By day, the streets were full of colour and life, from the fruit stalls, to the clothing mannequins, from the idle shoppers traipsing with their whining children, to the buskers strumming clumsily at the guitar.

But, by night the streets were emptied, because the soul of the town had been stripped out of it, by glass fronted stores, fast food outlets, and coffee shops. No one lived here, except the homeless on their cardboard mattresses in abandoned doorways. Silence.

Highlight the different contrasts in the example below.

Or age:

He felt his hip twinge, which on its own was bearable, but as his knees were already filled with gravel, and his knuckles filled with crushed glass, he looked for a park bench to rest at. At last, uncomfortably damp with sweat, even in this bitter cold, he sat and propped his stick at his side.

As the pain eased, he opened his eyes. Young mothers strolled across the park, some of them striding even in heels, while their children shot off, left and right, only to return like boomerangs, screaming with happiness and youth.

Memories of his young summers came back to him, and one morning, lying in the barley field with his eyes half shut in the sunshine. When, through the swaying stalks, her red dress flashed to him like a beacon, and Susan entered his life. She changed it forever.

- Did you notice how his pain is contrasted with the free, easy movement of the mothers and their children?
- How his slowness contrasts with the speed of the children.
- How he doesn't make a sound through his pain, but the children are screaming.
- That this scream is ironic – the children are expressing joy.
- How he is hot and sweating, even though the day is cold.
- How his memory takes him back to his youth, but also to a contrasting season, summer.
- How rest in the present old age is to stop the pain, whereas in his memory it was carefree, lying in the sunshine.

Notice how these contrasts of time and age are easy to plan in advance of the exam. You know that you can describe any scene given to you in different times or seasons, or moments in history.

Similarly, it is easy to describe a character at different ages, or contrasting them with other characters of different ages.

The next technique I'd like you to notice is the power of the list. Here the contrasts are built up through listed descriptions.

From *Antic Hay* by Aldous Huxley

Gumbril lived in a tall, narrow-shouldered, rickety house in a little obscure square not far from Paddington. There were five floors, and a basement with beetles, and nearly a hundred stairs, which shook when someone ran on them. Gumbrils's running days were gone, though. The house was prematurely old and decaying in a part of town which was declining rapidly.

The houses which a few years ago had all been occupied by respectable families, were now split up into squalid little apartments, and from the neighbouring slums, invading bands of children battled on the once sacred pavements.

Mr. Gumbril was almost the last survivor of the old inhabitants, because he loved his garden and the fourteen elm trees which welcomed the starlings who came, every evening in summer-time, to roost in their branches.

He used to sit out on his balcony waiting for the coming of the birds. And just at sunset, when the sky was most golden, there would be a twittering overhead, and the black, innumerable flocks of starlings would come sweeping across the sky to roost in his trees.

There were plenty of larger and leafier gardens all round; but they remained birdless, while every evening, a faithful legion of starlings settled clamorously among his trees. They sat and chattered till the sun went down and twilight was over.

Silence fell suddenly and inexplicably on all the birds at once, lasted a few seconds of thrilling suspense, before erupting in an outburst of the same loud and simultaneous conversation.

The starlings were Mr. Gumbril's most cherished friends. Sitting out on his balcony to watch and listen to them, he had caught many colds and chills. Yet he was always visible in the twilight, sitting on the balcony, gazing up, round-spectacled and rapt, at the fourteen elm trees.

While the birds chattered, he sat silently. His bony hand would clutch at his thin grey beard, stroking until darkness came and the starlings rejoined their flocks.

Answers to find the contrast

From *Antic Hay* by Aldous Huxley

Gumbril lived in a tall, narrow-shouldered, rickety house in a little obscure square not far from Paddington. **There were five floors, and a basement with beetles**, and **nearly a hundred stairs, which shook when someone ran on them**. Gumbrils's running days were gone, though. The house was prematurely old and decaying in a part of town which was declining rapidly.

The houses which a few years ago had all been occupied by respectable families, were now split up into squalid little apartments, and from the neighbouring slums, **invading bands of children battled on the once sacred pavements.**

Mr. Gumbril was almost **the last survivor** of the old inhabitants, because he loved his garden and the **fourteen elm trees** which welcomed the **starlings** who came, every evening in summer-time, to roost in their branches.

He used to **sit** out on his balcony **waiting** for the **coming of the birds**. And just at sunset, when the sky was most **golden**, there would be a twittering overhead, and the **black**, innumerable flocks of starlings would come sweeping across the sky to roost in his trees.

There were plenty of **larger and leafier gardens all round; but they remained birdless**, while every evening, a faithful **legion of starlings settled** clamorously among his trees. They sat and **chattered till the sun went down and twilight was over**.

Silence fell suddenly and inexplicably on all the birds at once, lasted a few seconds of **thrilling suspense, before erupting** in an outburst of the same loud and simultaneous conversation.

The starlings were Mr. Gumbril's most **cherished friends**. Sitting out on his balcony to watch and listen to them, he had **caught many colds and chills**. Yet he was always visible in the twilight, sitting on the balcony, gazing up, round-spectacled and rapt, at the fourteen elm trees.

While the birds chattered, he sat silently. His bony hand would clutch at his thin grey beard, stroking until darkness came and the starlings rejoined their flocks.

How Contrast Creates Drama in *Antic Hay*

- Five floors suggest grandeur, but the basement of beetles suggests decay.
- The hundred stairs suggest a substantial property, but they appear fragile because they shook when someone ran on them.
- The houses had once been respectable, and large, but now they have been split up into squalid little apartments.
- The children's battles are violent, and they are portrayed as invaders, which contrasts with the pavements which had once been sacred, and presumably peaceful and quiet.
- Mr Gumbril is a sole and last survivor, contrasted to the fourteen Elm trees and the many starlings.
- When the starlings arrive they are black, while the evening is golden.
- These contrasts use the house as a metaphor for Gumbril himself. Both are decaying, both were once grand and strong. Both are edging closer to darkness and death.
- However, the contrasts also give us a sense of hope, with life continuing, through the beetles, the Elm trees and the starlings. Rather than the sunset appearing threatening and symbolic of death, it is golden and symbolic of hope.
- This is backed up by the contrast of his garden to the birdless gardens of his neighbours.
- The contrast of silence with the excited chattering of the starlings suggests there is something special about Mr Gumbril.

I hope you can see that every description is framed around the contrast. Contrasts help you control the reader's reaction to your characters and events. They also add drama to any description, so that the reader is pushed along rather than sitting there scratching their heads wondering why the writer has spent so much time describing stuff pointlessly.

Using Imagery

Simile

How to Choose a Good Comparison for Your Simile

Smiles compare two things.

A really good simile has more than one point of comparison.

For example, in a previous description we met the simile: **"her red dress flashed to him like a beacon."**

The Points of Comparison
- One reason for the comparison is that a beacon can also be red.
- It can also flash. But so does a traffic light, or a neon light. A beacon will be lit by a flame though, so the simile also includes some movement, which fits the woman walking toward him much better than a light.
- Finally, a beacon is either lit as a guide, or a warning. This works because the reader is already primed for the idea of 'change'. We wonder if Susan will be a dangerous interruption to his life, or an improvement on his life before.

Similes are there to give you, not just a picture, but a **better** picture. They try to tell you as much as possible with as few words.

Examples of Developed Similes

Patches of snow lay on the grass like gloves.

Patches of snow lay on the grass like ladies' forgotten gloves.

Simple: She entered the fight like some huge chicken.
Developed: She entered the fight like some huge awkward chicken, torn, squawking, out of its coop.

Simple: She was obsessed with him, like a locked door with no key.
Developed: She was obsessed by the mystery of him and her curiosity infuriated her. He was like a door which had no lock and no key.

Simple: The pensioners tilted like towers of Pisa.
Developed: The elegant pensioners, leaning on their canes, tilted towards me like towers of Pisa.

Simple: The view of the city felt flat as a poster.
Developed: Outside, the teeming life of the city hung in my window, flat as a poster.

Simple: I hate jazz; it is like being chased by bees.

Developed: I hate jazz. The shrill trumpets feel like being chased by bees.

Work out how much extra information each developed simile gives you. That extra is also managed with just a few words. Remember, none of these are just to prove I am describing, they are there because I believe the **information** is important for a reader to know.

Cliché Similes

Typical mistakes with similes usually happen when you use 'as' rather than 'like'.

A mistake with a simile is choosing something most readers have heard before, many times. This makes it a cliché.

Examples of Cliché
- As fast as a cheetah, a racing car, a drum
- As loud as thunder, a drum
- As fierce as a lion
- As quiet as a mouse
- As cute as a kitten
- As happy as a clam
- As light as a feather
- As blind as a bat
- As bold as brass
- As bright as a button
- As shiny as a new pin
- As cold as ice
- As common as dirt
- As cool as a cucumber
- As hard as nails
- As hot as hell
- As innocent as a lamb
- As tall as a giraffe
- As tough as nails
- As white as a ghost
- As sweet as sugar
- As black as coal

So, be original. Try to use **like**, instead of **as**.

Write 5 interesting similes about any of the following:
1. Autumn in a place you have been to
2. A road you know
3. A child at a restaurant
4. A dog on a walk
5. A grandmother or grandfather on holiday
6. An old car

7. A ship caught in a storm
8. A computer crashing
9. A vain person on Instagram
10. A polar bear hunting a seal

Using Metaphor

Metaphors: What are they and why do we need them?

A metaphor compares two things, just as a simile does.
But it doesn't use 'as' or 'like'.
So, a metaphor says something *is* something else.

The trick is to find some characteristics in common between both things.

Here are some metaphors we have already met:
1. A **faithful legion** of starlings settled clamorously among his trees.
2. The starlings were Mr. Gumbril's most **cherished friends.**
3. But, by night the streets were emptied, because **the soul** of the town had been stripped out of it.
4. His knees were already **filled with gravel**, and his knuckles **filled with crushed glass**.

A metaphor tires to get you to see something familiar in a different way.
1. A legion is a group of soldiers, who are faithful to Mr Gumbril. It suggests that they are helping him in a battle - with old age, or memory, or the neighbourhood changing.
2. The starlings are cherished friends, which suggests how much Mr Gumbril looks forward to seeing them, and also implies that he must be incredibly lonely as they may have replaced human friends.
3. The town is dying, both spiritually and literally if it has lost its soul. Because the soul has been torn out, this is the fault of town planners, or business owners, rather than the citizens who live there.
4. Filling knees with gravel and knuckles with cut glass shows how much pain he must be in to use these joints. They also have a rough, gritty texture, which will draw blood, so they are linked. I could have filled his knuckles with needles, which would still give the idea of pain. But it wouldn't give me the same feeling of rough, gritty granules which I already have with gravel.

Make 3 notes about what you have learned about metaphors:
1. _____
2. _____
3. _____

Take a look at this photograph:

You might know the tower is called Big Ben, but it doesn't matter if you don't.

Let's Develop Metaphors in 5 Steps
1. Start with the verbs. What is the tower doing?
Standing, looking, telling the time, pointing, guarding.

2. What else does some or all of those things?
A tour guide, a soldier on guard, a parent, someone standing in a queue.

3. Start by comparing the two lists and writing a descriptive sentence.
Big Ben still stands on parade, proudly announcing that this is London.

4. Include other ideas in the image which will fit this idea. So, the red bus and the red telephone box stand out. I need to match the metaphors. It would be no good making the telephone box into a cat, or the bus into a boat. I need them to fit with the idea of Big Ben as someone old and on parade.

Big Ben still stands on parade, elegant even in old age. He is flanked by other ancient helpers. The red bus still gets about a bit, despite her age. The red telephone box is still here, waving at the passing tourist but, now everyone has a mobile phone, he's just a shell of his former self. Perhaps dementia has already set in.

Notice how the telephone box and the bus both have to behave in ways that show they are also like an old person. Linking your metaphors in this way feels much more satisfying for the reader, as it helps them see something familiar in a new way.

5. Make sure your **verbs** still work, for both things in the pair you are describing.

Big Ben still stands on parade, elegant even in old age. He is flanked by other ancient helpers. The red bus still gets about a bit, despite her age. The red telephone box is still here, waving at the passing tourist but, now everyone has a mobile phone, he's just a shell of his former self. Perhaps dementia has already set in.

Flanked describes them being on either side, so it is accurate. It is also associated with soldiers - to flank is to manoeuvre around the sides of your enemy - so it fits with the military idea of a **parade**.

Buses go places, and a phrase to describe a person doing this is **gets about**. If I had written 'travels' this would sound a lot like a bus, but only a little like a person. I want it to fit both equally well.

The idea of the phone box **waving** allows me to suggest that it is trying to attract attention - this works because it is red, and a symbol of tourist London. It also suggests that the phone box is a little desperate for attention. This works because no one needs to use it now.

Write down 3 things which you have learned about metaphors which will help you write better metaphors in your description.

1. _____
2. _____
3. _____

Seeing in Metaphor

Find the Metaphors

1. Read through this description of Autumn, mostly written in metaphor.
2. Highlight the metaphors which you find. (There are at least 30)

Autumn bustles her way into the park, calling to the strolling mothers, too young for school.

The silent bandstand longs for music, but the chatting mothers, dazed by sunlight, slip by.

The aged trees perform a guard of honour as autumn marries summer.

They send confetti in a shower of leaves. The ground is rusted gold.

A toddler smacks at the shimmering air.

The trees are stripping slowly, as autumn prepares her honeymoon.

Summer lifts a veil of sunlight, catching the lace of spider web, ready to kiss the morning.

Ornamental trees dazzle, blood red, rich and ripening.

Your spirits lift your gaze to a kaleidoscope of greens.

The park spins under your heel. A dizziness of colours, until the concrete paths break nature's spell.

The toddler is smacking squirrels who have fled.

A storm of leaves arrives like snowfall without winter's sting. Now the leaves turn to dry rain.

Amazed, you look up to a cloudless sky. Bushes reach out to you, blood red berries in their palms.

Shadows spring like roots at your feet, and you are painted in silhouette in the dying leaves.

The tall trees steal summer's generous warmth.

Squirrels also plunder the rusting ground, scampering away with gold, climbing like burglars onto rooftops, where they wait unseen.

The green trees show off their leaves. Another squirrel scurries to the sky.

An old dog plods, too tired to chase.

Young families glide by, still in the springtime of youth.

You notice a tree, gashed and weeping: a delta of sap spills out.

Sunlight or shadow? Which will win?

The old dog plods on, in an aimless circle, while the bandstand's clock ticks toward twelve.

Something is ending.

A child's picture book flutters on a park bench, commemorating the dead.

Time has cut down other giants, and centenarian trees gaze at the sawn down stump.

Ranks of benches line the route, each a life well lived or lost.

Sunshine or shadow? Which will win?

The flower beds still grow, some unfurling flags of colour, celebrating the sun.

The ornamental pond springs to life, and the sky peers into its murky mirror.

A prison riot of birds protest their innocence behind bars, free from cats and the coming winter. Are the bars better than cold and risk?

The fountain froths icing onto its wedding cake layers. It's ripples beat a shimmering circle and a floating filigree of light.

The park keeper's cottage is hidden in the bushes, like a character in fairy tale. A warning of a modern plague stands at one wall.

A dead carpet of leaves sees you home.

435 Words

Answers to Metaphor Hunt

1. Metaphors are in bold. Where there is more than one metaphor on a line, the second is highlighted in italics.

Autumn bustles her way into the park, calling to the strolling mothers, too young for school.

The silent bandstand longs for music, but the chatting mothers, dazed by sunlight, slip by.

The aged trees perform a guard of honour *as autumn marries summer.*

They send confetti in a shower of leaves. **The ground is rusted gold.**

A toddler smacks at the shimmering air.

The trees are stripping slowly, *as autumn prepares her honeymoon.*

Summer lifts a veil of sunlight, *catching the lace of spider web*, **ready to kiss the morning.**

Ornamental trees dazzle, blood red, rich and ripening.

Your spirits lift your gaze **to a kaleidoscope of greens.**

The park spins under your heel. A dizziness of colours, until the concrete paths **break nature's spell.**

The toddler is smacking squirrels who have fled.

A storm of leaves arrives like snowfall without winter's sting. **Now the leaves turn to dry rain.**

Amazed, you look up to a cloudless sky. **Bushes reach out to you, blood red berries in their palms.**

Shadows spring like roots at your feet, and y**ou are painted in silhouette** in the dying leaves.

The tall trees steal summer's generous warmth.

Squirrels also plunder the rusting ground, *scampering away with gold,* climbing like burglars onto rooftops, where they wait unseen.

The green trees show off their leaves. Another squirrel scurries to the sky.

An old dog plods, too tired to chase.

Young families glide by, **still in the springtime of youth.**

You notice a tree, gashed and *weeping:* **a delta of sap spills out.**

Sunlight or shadow? Which will win?

The old dog plods on, in an aimless circle, while the bandstand's clock ticks toward twelve.

Something is ending.

A child's picture book flutters on a park bench, commemorating the dead.

Time has cut down other giants, **and centenarian trees gaze at the sawn down stump.**

Ranks of benches line the route, each a life well lived or lost.

Sunshine or shadow? Which will win?

The flower beds still grow, **some unfurling flags of colour, celebrating the sun.**

The ornamental pond springs to life, and **the sky peers into its murky mirror.**

A prison riot of birds protest their innocence behind bars, free from cats and the coming winter. Are the bars better than cold and risk?

The fountain froths icing onto its wedding cake layers. Its ripples beat a shimmering circle and **a floating filigree of light**.

The park keeper's cottage is hidden in the bushes, like a character in fairy tale. A warning of a modern plague stands at one wall.

A dead carpet of leaves sees you home.

What to learn from this:

1. The description is simply a journey through the park, so a structure naturally happens – with the last line leading the reader back to the beginning.

2. To train my eye to see, I took my phone with me and filmed everything I looked at for 2-5 seconds. When I got home, I simply wrote a description of each clip, comparing what was in it to something else.

Take your phone and try it for yourself, filming 10 scenes or moments on a walk.

Using Extended Metaphor

Practising the extended metaphor is not easy. But, if you get it right, it adds at least grade 7 quality to your writing. If you get it wrong, it will add grade 6 quality to your writing. So, give it a go.

First focus on what your subject (the thing you want to describe) does. It might help you to quickly write a list of everything you picture it doing. Verbs, as always, are your building blocks.

After a minute, look at your list of actions, and ask yourself this question: "what else does something similar?" This will give you the thing to compare it to, (let's call it the object).

Now try to jot down as many things about their appearance as possible. Start with the subject. Each time, see if you can compare it to something about the appearance of the object.

Once you have two or more ideas, you can begin writing.

Remember, you don't have to write metaphors as long and detailed as mine. One comparison will still give you a metaphor! Two or three will mark you out as having more skill than a normal student. It is such an easy way to get the top grades, once you have a few in the bank.

Example in Action

So, let's imagine I have to describe a car as a cow.

Start by listing the verbs that cars do:

Race, drive, turn, park, overtake, brake, carry, roar.

Now think of the appearance of a car. What does it have that I might describe with words associated with a cow?

Make a list.

- They both have horns, and can bellow.
- Horns are at the top of a cow, and cars can have roof racks on their tops.
- What do they have at their sides? Cows have ears, and cars have wing mirrors.
- The car's exterior could be a hide, and its colours could be markings.
- Cars have grills, which can be like faces, and lights can be eyes.
- The exhaust is at the back, and expels pollutants, and the cow expels cow pats and methane from its back.
- They are both bigger than people.
- Cows walk to their feeding in a line, which is like cars on a road.
- Cows would halt at a feeding station. Cars halt when parking, or at traffic lights.

Ok, now I have thought really hard about cars, and cows, I just need to put bits together. I just need to think of when I would want to describe a car as a cow. Well, it wouldn't be a compliment. So it could be a second-hand car, which is all I can afford, or a rental car, which is all that is available.

A Car: As a Cow

The car was parked at an odd angle, as though grazing at the grassy verge. Its grill flashed silver teeth in a threatening, bovine* smile.

The wing mirrors stuck out horribly, like twitching ears, while the roof rack pointed from its head with ungainly horns.

I knew the moment I rented it, that this lump of a car would probably handle like a cow, trundling and squirting out methane on the country lane.

I was in a hurry, so pumped the accelerator like an impatient milkmaid squeezing every last drop. But it was old and knackered, and wouldn't deliver any more.

*Like a cow, usually meaning 'stupid' like a cow.

Task:

Write down 5 bullet points to summarise what you have learned about extended metaphors.

1. _____
2. _____
3. _____
4. _____
5. _____

More Extended Metaphor Examples

- These extended metaphors are organised approximately in order of difficulty and complexity.
- The idea is to help you see how even a short extended metaphor brings a lot to your writing.
- And then how you can develop these in more depth.

An Old Face and farmed fields

Her face was textured and rough, an ancient field folded by the plough, carved deeply with mediaeval furrows, and perhaps the promise of buried treasure. The plenty and promise of spring and the green sap of youth had left it, and now its ridges cracked and browned beneath a greying sky.

A Young Face and a perfect beach

She watched his young face and was reminded of a perfect holiday. The pools of his eyes were calm, a flickering of emerald and aquamarine. They were a perfect painting of warm waters, undisturbed at the breaking day.

His bright, white smile stretched before her in a gentle curve, a warm and welcoming beach, still fresh, still unmarked by time, still on show only for her.

The Sea: as a horse race, with surfers as jockeys

The waves galloped towards the shore, their white manes fluffed and frothing with the effort. The supple surfers, holding on for dear life, even their toes gripping on desperately and with the sheer thrill of the movement, rode the waves. They crested the jumps as the waves barrelled forward, charging with greater hoofbeats and a hotter breath as they broke towards the sandy finish line.

Giraffes at a Zoo: as soldiers, officers, in uniform.

The giraffes stand like sentinels*, tired and slow. Their necks swing in slow motion, as though they are on parade in an uncomfortable heat. And yet, they have brushed up well. Their coats shine, and the intricate pattern of diamonds and hexagons and parallelograms knit together perfectly. Worn with pride. They salute each other like officers at the mess*, before they tuck in to a three course meal.

Outside the cages, the civilians come and go. Their markings are drab, and they smell of ice cream, sun creams, face creams. People are artificial, loud and fake. How would they cope in the real world, behind bars?

As though hearing a secret order, the animals about-face and return to quarters, ready for mess.

*guards, on look out, or on watch

*mess is where soldiers have their meals

The Storm: as a famous actress delivering a melodramatic performance

We watched the Diva prepare for her final scene, first flouncing in the distance, flinging clouds before her in her frustration. The sky rushed to escaper her, chased away by her reddening mood. She had changed now into a purple and black number, with endless folds wrapping themselves around the horizon, while she began to scream out the lines. Yes, we had heard this stormy script before, but never delivered with such rage and passionate force.

We stood on the hill top, in the best seats in the house, and prepared for the performance of a lifetime. As the sun set, the stage lights cracked and thundered into life, and jagged streaks like fire, like mercury, like a standing ovation, announced her sudden entrance on the stage from behind a curtain of hail.

The City: As a Computer Loading the Internet

Damn it, the early morning traffic was buffering again, stuck on an endless loop. Drivers sought to distract themselves, risking a quick glance at their phones, while the day uploaded, and the sun began to spin towards the centre of their windscreens.

The suburbs sprang disappointingly to life: pages that should have been shut down the night before, but here they were, loading again and again, adding yet more delay.

And then, finally, the city grew grander, and the sky scrapers Googled the white space of the sky, beautiful, searching the heavens for answers.

Their frustrations eased, the commuters left their cars behind; a final click of their electronic keys, and here they were, ready for work, pressing with relief at the elevator buttons. Send.

What You Should do Now

1. Write your own extended metaphor.
2. Make it between 50 and 100 words.
3. Remember the 5 steps of building a metaphor - go back to Lesson 33 if you have forgotten.

You can write about anything. However, if you are stuck, compare one thing from each column (they don't have to be on the same row):

Ship	Elephant
Church	Mother
Airport	Computer
Sports stadium	Holiday
Your house	Car crash
A vehicle	Baby

How to Use the Senses

The Senses: Sound and Smell

You have probably been taught to write about the senses in your description. Real writers don't think this way.

Instead they think visually first - that's why we have looked at so much visual imagery: contrast, simile and metaphor, personification and extended metaphor.

These will inevitably involve the senses.

Let's go back to the last section to take a look:

An Old Face and farmed fields

> Her face was **textured** and **rough**, an ancient field folded by the plough, **carved deeply** with mediaeval furrows, and perhaps the promise of buried treasure. The plenty and promise of spring and the green sap of youth had left it, and now **its ridges cracked and browned** beneath a greying sky.

In bold, you can see all the textures which the reader can interpret through the sense of touch. But I have never made any character touch them, nor told you what they would feel like to touch. This would be clumsy, and just be there to prove I am using the senses. Instead, I write a **visual** description which helps the reader *imagine* what the texture would feel like.

A Young Face and a perfect beach

> She watched his young face and was reminded of a perfect holiday. The pools of his eyes were **calm**, a flickering of emerald and aquamarine. They were a perfect painting of **warm waters**, undisturbed at the breaking day.
>
> His bright, white smile stretched before her in a **gentle curve, a warm and welcoming** beach, still fresh, still unmarked by time, still on show only for her.

In bold, we have words you would associate with touch. But crucially no touching actually happens, as that would be clumsy.

The Sea: as a horse race, with surfers as jockeys

> The waves **galloped** towards the shore, their white manes fluffed and **frothing** with the effort.
>
> The supple surfers, holding on for dear life, even their toes gripping on desperately and with the sheer thrill of the movement, rode the waves. They crested the jumps as the waves **barrelled** forward, charging with **greater hoofbeats** and a hotter breath as they broke towards the sandy finish line.

In bold are words we might associate with sound. But I never tell the reader what the sounds are. Another way of thinking about the senses is that they should be *shown*, not *told*.

Remember that writers don't like to tell you what things smelt like, or sounded like. They don't write about their characters touching things, and get you understand what they felt like by telling you.

Instead they use words which suggest texture and suggest sound. They let the reader add up 2 + 2.

How to Use the Sense of Smell

Writers make us aware of smell, without always having to describe it. Here is an extract from **Ulysses**, by James Joyce. It is an incredibly famous book, but hardly anyone has read it, because it is so long, and so detailed.

That's great news for us, though, because it is packed with description. Here is an extract where a dog is loose on the beach and comes across the corpse of another dog, washed up on the sand.

> The carcass lay on his path. He stopped, **sniffed,** stalked round it, his brother dog, **nosing closer**, went round it again, **sniffling rapidly** like a dog all over the dead dog's bedraggled body.
>
> "Fenton*!* Out of that, you mongrel*!*"
>
> The **cry** brought him skulking back to his master and a blunt, barefoot kick sent him unscathed across a spit of sand, crouched in flight. He slunk back in a curve. Along by the edge of the wall he lolloped, dawdled, **smelt a rock** and from under a cocked hindleg *__pissed__* against it. He trotted forward and, lifting again his hindleg, *__pissed__* quick short bursts at an **unsmelt rock**. Simple pleasures. His hind paws then scattered the sand: his forepaws dabbled and delved. Something he buried there. He rooted in the sand, dabbling, delving and stopped *__to listen to the air__*, *__scraped__* up the sand again with *__a fury of his claws__*, then ceased, standing like a vicar presiding over a burial, vulturing the dead.
>
> The carcass lay on his path. He stopped, **sniffed**, stalked round it, his brother dog, **nosing closer**, went round it again, **sniffling rapidly** like a dog all over the dead dog's bedraggled body.
>
> "Fenton! Out of that, you mongrel!"
>
> The **cry** brought him skulking back to his master and a blunt, barefoot kick sent him unscathed across a spit of sand, crouched in flight. He slunk back in a curve. Along by the edge of the wall he lolloped, dawdled, **smelt a rock** and from under a cocked hindleg **pissed** against it. He trotted forward and, lifting again his hindleg, **pissed** quick short bursts at an **unsmelt rock**. Simple pleasures. His hind paws then scattered the sand: his forepaws dabbled and delved. Something he buried there. He rooted in the sand, dabbling, delving and stopped **to listen to the air**, **scraped** up the sand again with a **fury of his claws**, then ceased, standing like a vicar presiding over a burial, vulturing the dead.

How easy it would be to describe the smell of a dead dog, or the smell of the pissing. But there is no need.

Look at the words in bold. The repetition of 'sniff' makes us imagine the smell. The repetition of 'pissed' reminds us of a smell we all know already.

Sound and the Sense of Hearing

In later sections, we will look at the impact of alliteration, sibilance and assonance in focusing the reader's ear on sounds. But for now, look at all the words highlighted in italics and bold. These all tell us that sound is happening, without trying to describe the individual sounds to us. The exclamation marks tell us about loudness, too.

This is another example of showing, not telling. It is letting the reader add 2 + 2 to get 4.

Why do Teachers Train You to Use the Senses?

Writers use the senses all the time. Many teachers, perhaps, are not teaching description based on what good writers actually do. In other words, writers don't usually try to *tell* us about the senses. They try to *show* us.

Teachers are teaching techniques which they hope will get you through the exam. But in this instance, it is training you to do the wrong thing, because you are likely to tell the reader what things feel, sound and smell like.

You will get top grades by describing as real writers do.

Charles Dickens - a master of description.

Here is Charles Dickens, describing food for sale at Christmas in **A Christmas Carol**:

> There were great, round, pot-bellied baskets of chestnuts, shaped like the waistcoats of jolly old gentlemen, lolling at the doors, and tumbling out into the street in their apoplectic opulence. There were ruddy, brown-faced, broad-girthed Spanish Onions, shining in the fatness of their growth like Spanish Friars, and winking from their shelves in wanton slyness at the girls as they went by, and glanced demurely at the hung-up mistletoe. There were pears and apples, clustered high in blooming pyramids; there were bunches of grapes, made, in the shopkeepers' benevolence to dangle from conspicuous hooks, **that people's mouths might water** gratis as they passed; there were piles of filberts, mossy and brown, recalling, ***in their fragrance, ancient walks among the woods, and pleasant shufflings ankle deep through withered leaves***; there were Norfolk Biffins, squat and swarthy, setting off the yellow of the oranges and lemons, and, in the great compactness of their **juicy** persons, urgently entreating and beseeching to be carried home in paper bags and eaten after dinner.

Notice that the bold references are references to tastes, but those tastes are not actually described.

The smell is very cleverly done in bold italics. Instead of describing the smell itself, he describes a memory the reader might have of being in the countryside. A memory they associate with a smell.

This is so clever because, out of all the senses, smell has the strongest relationship with memory for all of us.

Quiz yourself:

1. Which sense do writers pay most attention to?
    - Visual
    - Auditory (sound)
    - Smell
    - Taste

2. In what we have seen, writers associate taste with?
    - memory
    - flavour

3. Writers tell us about sound by:
    - Telling us what the sound sounds like - telling
    - Using words which suggest a sound – showing

Answers: **sound, memory, showing**.

What Dickens Teaches Us About Smell

A Tale of Two Cities, by Charles Dickens

I searched the whole of this novel for these words:

smell, smelt, odour, nostril, nose, aroma, stench, whiff

These are virtually the whole number of *specific* descriptions of smell in the whole novel. There are ONLY 8. So, describing smells *directly* is very rare.. Dickens is a great writer, so he uses the 'show don't tell' method. I've picked on these moments of '*tell*' to *show* that, even when he is *telling* the reader, he still relies on 'show'. Words in italics are the '*show*'. Words in bold are the *tell*.

1. The *mildewy* inside of the coach, with its **damp** and dirty straw, its disagreeable **smell**, and its obscurity, was rather like a larger dog-kennel.

2. A narrow winding street, full of offence and **stench**, with other narrow winding streets diverging, all peopled by rags and nightcaps, and all **smelling of rags and nightcaps**, and all visible things with a brooding look upon them that looked ill.

3. The night was hot, and the shop, close shut and surrounded by *so foul a neighbourhood*, **was ill-smelling**. Monsieur Defarge's olfactory sense was by no means delicate, but the **stock of wine smelt** *much stronger than it ever tasted*, and so did the stock of rum and brandy and aniseed. *He whiffed the compound of scents away*, as he put down *his smoked-out pipe*.

4. He accompanied his conductor into a guard-room**, smelling of common wine and tobacco**, where certain soldiers and patriots, asleep and awake, drunk and sober, and in various neutral states between sleeping and waking, drunkenness and sobriety, were standing and lying about.

5. Your bank-notes had a **musty odour**, as if they were *fast decomposing* into rags again.

6. The carriage was 'swinging and lumbering upward among the many **sweet scents of a summer night**'.

7. **The sweet scents of the summer night** rose all around him, and rose, as the rain falls, impartially, on the *dusty*, ragged, and toil-worn group at the fountain not far away

8. The sight and **scent of flowers** in the City streets had some **waifs of goodness** in them.

Even when Dickens just comes out and tells us what a smell is, he still uses a large number of words which help us imagine the smell *indirectly*, without describing it, like 'mildewy', 'damp', 'dusty' - there may be hundreds of examples of this sort of description where the reader adds up 2 + 2.

Here's something else great writers almost never do when they are describing smells. They try to avoid using these two words: **nose, nostrils**. Those words are telling, and of course the reader is 100% likely to guess that if there is a smell, the character used their nose and nostrils to detect it!

Write down 3 things you have learned about describing smells in your writing.
1._____
2._____
3._____

What Dickens Teaches Us About Sound

<u>**Oliver Twist, By Charles Dickens**</u>

Extract 1
"Stop thief! Stop thief!" There is a magic in the sound. The tradesman leaves his counter, and the car-man his waggon; the butcher throws down his tray; the baker his basket; the milkman his pail; the errand-boy his parcels; the school-boy his marbles; the paviour his pickaxe; the child his battledore.

Away they run, pell-mell, helter-skelter, slap-dash: tearing, yelling, screaming, knocking down the passengers as they turn the corners, rousing up the dogs, and astonishing the fowls: and streets, squares, and courts, re-echo with the sound.

Write down three things you learn about suggesting noise.
1._____
2._____
3._____

Answers
- "Stop thief! Stop thief!" – we can tell the urgency and loudness of the sound through the exclamation mark.
- **There is a magic in the sound. The tradesman leaves his counter, and the car-man his waggon**; - we imagine the instant effect of the sound, the shouting, which has stopped everything. Then Dickens introduces his favourite descriptive technique, the detailed, list which introduces layers of action.
- **the butcher throws down his tray; the baker his basket; the milkman his pail;** - notice that these actions, and particularly the tray and pail, force us to imagine harsh sounds – there is not need to tell us what the sounds are.
- **the errand-boy his parcels; the school-boy his marbles; the paviour his pickaxe; the child his battledore.** – and here go goes again – exactly the same idea, but this time with the brilliant addition of marbles clattering. Why didn't he tell us they clattered? Because he uses 'show don't tell'!
- **Away they run, pell-mell, helter-skelter, slap-dash:** - now the list itself works as onomatopoeia, recreating sounds for us.
- **tearing, yelling, screaming, knocking down the passengers as they turn the corners,** - these are all things we would hear. He simply lets us work out for ourselves what the sound would be while he shows us what we would see.
- **rousing up the dogs, and astonishing the fowls:** - another list to show us other causes of noise.
- **and streets, squares, and courts, re-echo with the sound.** – because he knows we are already thinking about all these sounds he ***hasn't described*** he can now tell us to imagine it with a "re-echo". He tells us what to do with the sounds, not what they are.

Extract 2
Oliver is walking to Smithfield market, London's largest livestock* market.

It was market-morning. The ground was covered, nearly ankle-deep, with filth and mire; a thick steam, perpetually rising from the reeking bodies of the cattle, and mingling with the fog, which seemed to rest upon the chimney-tops, hung heavily above.

1. Apart from 'reeking', what details suggests the smells of the market will be unpleasant?

Countrymen, butchers, drovers*, hawkers*, boys, thieves, idlers, and vagabonds* of every low grade, were mingled together in a mass; the whistling of drovers, the barking dogs, the bellowing and plunging of the oxen, the bleating of sheep, the grunting and squeaking of pigs, the cries of hawkers, the shouts, oaths, and quarrelling on all sides; the ringing of bells and roar of voices, that issued from every public-house*; the crowding, pushing, driving, beating, whooping and yelling; the hideous and discordant din that resounded from every corner of the market; and the unwashed, unshaven, squalid, and dirty figures constantly running to and fro, and bursting in and out of the throng*; rendered it a stunning and bewildering scene, which quite confounded the senses.

*livestock – a market for selling live animals
*drovers - men who lead cows
*hawkers – people who sell things in the streets
*vagabonds - tramps
*public-house - pub or bar
*throng - crowd

1. Make a list of all the words which suggest a sound.

2. Make 3-5 notes which will help you in your recreation of sounds:

   a. _____

   b. _____

   c. _____

   d. _____

   e. _____

3. Write your own description of a crowded place which uses the same words. If you are stuck, choose a train station, an airport, a shopping centre, a prison, a school dining hall or playground, a sporting event, a party...

Charles Dickens Oliver Twist

Let's look at how you might steal from other writers, in a way that isn't plagiarism.

Countrymen, butchers, drovers*, hawkers, boys, thieves, idlers, and vagabonds* of every low grade, were mingled together in a mass; the **whistling** of drovers, the **barking** dogs, the **bellowing** and **plunging** of the oxen, the **bleating** of sheep, the **grunting** and **squeaking** of pigs, the **cries** of hawkers, the **shouts, oaths,** and **quarrelling** on all sides; the **ringing of bells** and **roar of voices**, that issued from every public-house*; the **crowding, pushing, driving, beating, whooping and yelling**; the hideous and **discordant din** that **resounded from every corner** of the market; and the unwashed, unshaven, squalid, and dirty figures **constantly running to and fro**, and **bursting** in and out of the throng*; rendered it a stunning and bewildering scene, which quite confounded the senses.

Identify the Sound Words

Whistling	barking	bellowing	plunging	bleating	grunting
squeaking	cries	shouts	oaths	quarrelling	ringing
roar	Crowding	pushing	driving	beating	whooping
yelling	discordant	din	resounded	running	bursting

Now that I have these words, I am going to use them. I can write about anything of course, but I want to learn to write like a real writer. So, here I pick JK Rowling, and try to use these words in a paragraph which might fit into a Harry Potter book. Pick a book that you know.

Adapted for Harry Potter

Harry and Ron were late for the Hogwarts Express, and the **whistling** of the train's great engine came **ringing** down the platform as they ran, **bursting** through the crowded passengers. The progress of the Slitherin students could be guessed from the onslaught of **grunting, shouting, oaths and quarrelling** along the platform, as Malfoy and his admirers demanded the best carriage. The younger students were still **bleating** excitedly, **squeaking** in young voices, which reminded Harry of his own first trip. Then the **barking** and **bellowing** of the porters and train guards had felt like a **discordant din**, but now the **resounding** clamour made him feel entirely at home. They spotted Hermione and Ginny, pushing through a throng of sixth formers and Ron let out an embarrassing **whoop**.

If you don't like reading, or simply if you fancy a different challenge, use the words to write about a film or TV show.

Adapted for the TV show Friends

The party hadn't yet descended into **quarrelling**. Phoebe was singing about Smelly Cat again, a **discordant din** that somehow didn't make her any less attractive. Ross was drunk now, **bellowing** something about the T.Rex not having short arms, and **barking** at Monica that yes, palaeontology was a sexy science. Monica was in the kitchen again, keeping the party fed, **pushing** sausage rolls at the **bleating** crowd they knew from Central Perk. Joey could be heard **grunting** his way through a whole plate of spiced chicken wings, and mouthing **oaths** at Chandler who tried to steal one from his plate. **Whooping** as he succeeded, Chandler ran, **bursting** into the bathroom, where Janice found him, her **screaming**, **squeaky** voice **ringing** in his ears - something about Rachel being on a break.

Remember that we are not putting in every sound we can think of. We have to make sure the sounds fit the type of story we are writing. We have to imagine them in a book. If the reader ever feels one of these sounds is only included to prove we are describing, rather than to tell us something important, they will stop trusting us and the story we've written.

Creating a Soundscape

Writers have four main techniques for creating a soundscape, in addition to the Dickens style list. You need to know what these are, so that you can exploit them in your writing. The reason they are so important is that they show the reader what the sound is, rather than tell them.

When you use these **at the same time** you are layering sound upon sound. That's just what Dickens' list does. This is why I call it a soundscape. It is exactly how composers create music with more than one instrument playing at the same time.

Alliteration: repetition of consonant *sounds* at the *beginning* of words. '**The *cars careered* round the track, g-force gripping *tyres to the tarmac*, while their *drivers dared* to pass each other millimetres from *destruction and death*.**' Remember that the words must begin with the same sound. So '**g**-force **g**ripping' isn't alliteration, because the sounds of the 'g' are different. But 'it was always **fun** to **ph**one her **fr**iend' has three alliterative words, because 'phone' creates the same 'f' sound.

Consonance: repetition of consonants *anywhere* in words, usually linking with alliteration. Again, this needs to be for effect. For example, read this out loud and notice what pronouncing the 't's does to the mood of the description.

You notice a trail of light, leading from the jetty directly to the centre of the lake, where it widens like an open armed invitation. You imagine the sitter ought to stand, to scan the light for clues, to see the spotlight as it promises to illuminate the star turn. But the star is going to make a late entrance, evidently.

Did you notice that it forces you to enunciate, to really pronounce the 't'? This slows the reading down, it slows time down. It is also slightly harsh in sound, it puts us very slightly on edge. We're not entirely comfortable, as though we are worried about what is coming next.

Assonance: repetition of vowel sounds in words which are close together. This shouldn't be random, but to control the mood or speed of what you are describing. For example, "**I tried to make the kite fly**" emphasises the effort and possible failure. '**By the lake I saw "a host of golden daffodils"**' stretches out the syllables to create a sense of wonder.

Sibilance: repetition of letters which create the 's' or 'sh' sound. These are usually used to create either a soothing or a sinister tone, depending on the context. For example, a sinister version: "**the waves sucked at the wreck, and sailors clung to the sinking sides as the sharks circled.**" A soothing version: "**sands stretch across the shore, softly stroked by a murmuring surf**".

Fricatives: use of the 'f' sound. Although this can be used to create a soothing mood, it is much more likely to be used to show anger or contempt. This is because our mouths bare their teeth when we form the 'f' – this is part of our evolution to show aggression. Watch a chimp or a dog and you'll see the evolutionary link of 'f' to aggression.

Soothing example: "**for fun we crashed through the foaming waves, the white froth of the surf spinning from our bodies like lace.**"

Aggressive example: "**forget forgiveness. Rage filled her chest with fire. She felt like screaming but faced him silently instead, forcing her fear aside and replacing it with fury.**"

1. Repetition of the same letter or sound at the beginning of words which are close together is

- Alliteration
- Assonance
- Consonance
- Fricatives
- Sibilance

2. Alliteration includes sibilance

- True
- False

3. Consonance includes alliteration

- True
- False

4. The letters t, k, ck, p, d, g, and b are called plosives

- True
- False

5. The repetition of s or 'sh' sounds in words which are close together is

- Alliteration
- Assonance
- Consonance
- Fricatives
- Sibilance

6. Sibilance might not be alliteration

- True
- False

7. Consonance includes assonance

- True
- False

8. The sound produced by letters where you bare your teeth - F and V

- Alliteration
- Assonance
- Consonance
- Fricatives
- Sibilance

9. The repetition of vowels which share a similar sound in words which are close together

- Alliteration
- Assonance
- Consonance
- Fricatives
- Sibilance

10. The repetition of consonants which share a similar sound in words which are close together

- Alliteration
- Assonance
- Consonance
- Fricatives
- Sibilance

Answers: alliteration, true, true, true, sibilance, false, false, fricatives, assonance, consonance

Choosing Alliteration Which Works

1. Which works best?

   a) The barbarians broke through the barricade.
   b) He acts silly at times, but he was blessed with a brilliant brain.
   c) The beautiful bouquet blossomed in the bright sun.

2. Which works best?

   a) Despite their mother's warnings, the children chose to chew with their mouths open.
   b) The rich man was so cheap that it was chilling.
   c) The crowd cheered when the champion hit the challenger with a chair.

3. Which works best?

   a) Grass grows greener in the graveyard.
   b) The ghouls and ghosts greeted the gangly goblins.
   c) I reached under the desk and grabbed the gross gum.

4. Which one works best?

   a) Menacing sounds of mashing metal machines emanated from the mines.
   b) All of the millionaire's money only made him more melancholy.
   c) My mother makes a mouth-watering mincemeat pie.

Answers: always pick the one that feels natural, without any words chosen *just* so that they can alliterate. 1a, 2a, 3a, 4b

What Dickens Teaches Us About Harsh Sounds
From **A Christmas Carol** by Charles Dickens

Read this extract and highlight words which sound harsh when you say them out loud.

Oh! But he was a tight-fisted hand at the grindstone, Scrooge! a squeezing, wrenching, grasping, scraping, clutching, covetous, old sinner! Hard and sharp as flint, from which no steel had ever struck out generous fire; secret, and self-contained, and solitary as an oyster. The cold within him froze his old features, nipped his pointed nose, shrivelled his cheek, stiffened his gait; made his eyes red, his thin lips blue.

Answers to Harsh Sounds

Consonance

Oh! **But** he was a **tight-fisted** hand a**t** the **gr**indstone, Scrooge! a s**q**ueezing, wren**ch**ing, **gr**asping, **scr**aping, **cl**ut**ch**ing, **c**ovetous, old sinner! Har**d and** sharp as flint, from whi**ch** no steel ha**d** e**ver** s**tr**uck out generous fire; se**cr**et, **and** self-**c**on**t**ained, **and** solitary as **an** oys**ter**. The **c**old within him **fr**oze his **o**ld features, **nipped** his **po**inted **n**ose, shri**v**elled his **ch**eek, stiffe**ned** his **g**ait; ma**d**e his eyes **r**ed, his thin **l**ips blue.

Assonance

Oh! But he was a tight-fisted hand at the grindstone, Scrooge! a **squeezing, wrenching, grasping, scraping, clutching**, covetous, old sinner! Hard and sharp as flint, from which no steel had ever struck out generous fire; secret, and self-contained, and solitary as an oyster. The cold **within him froze his old features, nipped his** pointed nose, **shrivelled his cheek, stiffened his** gait; made his eyes red, **his thin lips** blue.

Fricatives

Oh! But he was a tight-fisted hand at the grindstone, Scrooge! a squeezing, wrenching, grasping, scraping, clutching, covetous, old sinner! Hard and sharp as flint, from which no steel had ever struck out generous fire; secret, and self-contained, and solitary as an oyster. The cold within him froze his old features, nipped his pointed nose, shrivelled his cheek, stiffened his gait; made his eyes red, his thin lips blue.

Sibilance

Oh! But he was a tight-fisted hand at the grind**stone, Scrooge! a squeezing**, wrenching, gra**sping**, **scr**aping, clutching, covetou**s, old sinner**! Hard and sharp as flint, from which no **steel** had ever **struck** out generou**s** fire; **secret,** and **sel**f-contained, and **solitary as an**

oyster. The cold within him froze hi**s** old feature**s**, nipped hi**s** pointed no**s**e, **sh**rivelled hi**s** cheek, stiffened his gait; made his eyes red, his thin lips blue.

What Dickens Teaches Us About Soft Sounds
From *David Copperfield*, by Charles Dickens

I came, one evening before suns**e**t, down into a v**a**lley, where I was to r**e**st. **I**n the course **o**f my desc**e**nt to **i**t, by the wind**i**ng tr**a**ck along the mountain-side, from which I saw **i**t shin**i**ng far below, I th**i**nk some long-**u**nw**o**nt**e**d s**e**nse **o**f beauty **a**nd tranquillity, some s**o**ften**i**ng **i**nfluence **a**wak**e**ned by its peace, moved faintly **i**n my breast.

99 vowels, 29 of which are hard (and do not say their own name). They are in bold.

I rem**e**mb**e**r pausing once, with a kind **o**f s**o**rrow th**a**t was n**o**t all **o**ppressive, n**o**t quite d**e**spairing. I rem**e**mber **a**lmost hoping th**a**t some b**e**tter change was p**o**ssible with**i**n me.

56 vowels, 26 of which are hard (and do not say their own name). They are in bold.

When you read these paragraphs out loud, you will hear the difference. The first sounds much softer. This is not an accident, because the soft sounds exactly match the feeling of "peace" and "tranquillity" Dickens is after.

In the second paragraph, the vowel sounds are much harsher. Again, this is deliberate, because the atmosphere needs to be nearly "oppressive".

Let's take a piece of Dickens and rewrite it to make the sounds softer.

Below is the original text, with the sibilance highlighted.

I came into the valley, **as the evening sun was shining on the remote heights of snow**, *that closed it in, like eternal clouds. The bases of the mountains forming the gorge in which the little village lay, were richly green; and high above this gentler vegetation, grew forests of dark fir, cleaving the wintry snow-drift, wedge-like, and stemming the avalanche.*

Above these, were range upon range of craggy steeps, grey rock, bright ice, and smooth verdure-specks of pasture, all gradually blending with the crowning snow. Dotted here and there on the mountain's-side, each tiny dot a home, were lonely wooden cottages, so dwarfed by the towering heights that they appeared too small for toys.

So did even the clustered village in the valley, with its wooden bridge across the stream, where the stream tumbled over broken rocks, and roared away among the trees. In the quiet air, **there was a sound of distant singing—shepherd voices;** *but, as one bright evening cloud floated midway along the mountain's-side, I could almost have believed it came from there, and was not earthly music.* **All at once, in this serenity, great Nature spoke to me; and soothed me** *to lay down my weary head upon the grass, and weep as I had not wept yet, since Dora died!*

Now the rewritten to emphasise soft sounds. Again sibilance is highlighted.

I came into the valley, as the evening **sun was shining on peaks of snow, encircling** *like clouds. The tiny village nestled on the rich green lower slopes of a gorge. Above, on* **steeper slopes, forests of dark fir split the snow drifts**, *wedging the weight of snow, and planted to* **stem avalanches.**

Above these, range upon range of craggy steeps, grey rock, bright **ice, and smooth green-specks of pasture**, *blended with the crowning snow. Lonely wooden cottages dotted the mountain side, dwarfed by the towering heights so they appeared too small even for toys.*

So did the clustered village in the valley, with its wooden bridge across the stream, where the stream tumbled over broken rocks, and roared away among the trees. In the quiet air, there **was a sound of distant singing—shepherd voices** *floating like mountain mist. All at* **once, in this serenity, nature spoke to me, and soothed me to lie down and rest upon the grass,** *and weep as I had not wept yet, since Dora died!*

- You only really learn from this by reading it out loud, to see the difference in soundscape.
- Focus on the vowels which say their own name.
- Focus also on the consonants which sound soft – sh, m, f, w, l.

Now you need to practise using this technique. Here's mine:

Writing Using Soft Sounds

Wives and mothers lead their excited families on the beach. Warm sand seeps between toes, worming its way inside shoes and flip-flops. They spread towels where the soft sand stiffens near the shore. Here, the children rush giggling out to the waves, leaping over the white froth which sweeps the beach with salt. Gently, the waves recede, their fingers stroking the bathers' legs, and sucking them further out.

- Did you notice the words that **show** sounds, **but don't tell** us the sound?
- Dickens has taught us to use the soft vowels which say their own name: A E I O U
- In addition, soft sounding consonants I have used are S, SH, W. Others are L, M, F.
- You will notice this creates a lot of sibilance which can always be used to create soft, soothing sounds.
- Sibilance is also used in an onomatopoeic way to recreate the sound of surf on the sand.
- Notice that there are 12 words that begin with W. Then look at how many words have the soft E sound. I count 9.

Answers to show don't tell: **rush, giggling, sucking.**

Journeys

To be brilliant at description, you have to make the whole thing work, from beginning to end. It can't just be there to prove to the examiner that you are describing. There has to be a reason for that description to exist – not just for the exam.

You need to think of description as it might appear in a novel, something you would choose to read. So how to you write 400-500 words in this way, without it appearing forced or fake?

Write the description as a journey. The journey will be through memories, or a place you know, or a picture in an art or photography gallery, or through an extended metaphor. A journey will make sure that your description is filled with a sense of action, even if very little happens.

Journeys Through Memory

This first example shows you my number one way to practise better writing. It is astonishingly simple. JUST START EACH SENTENCE WITH A DIFFERENT WORD. This one rule will force you to be creative, and to make each sentence interesting.

To build up to this, use the following approach. Follow the 15 instructions below. They don't have to be in that order – any order would work. They just force you to write interesting sentences.

Stage 1 – Start each sentence with a different word

1. Start with a verb
2. Start with an adverb
3. At least 25 words
4. Use a contrast
5. Start with although
6. Write a 5-word sentence
7. Use a simile
8. Start with perhaps
9. Use words with c, k, t in them
10. Use a metaphor
11. Use words with s, sc, sh in them
12. Include a texture
13. Include something gold or silver
14. Include a question
15. Refer back to an idea from the beginning, but show it as slightly different

Sample Exam Question

- Write about a person or place.
- The extra instruction inside your head: Every sentence must follow on from the last, so that the whole piece makes sense.

Mr Salles's Thought Process
- I asked my son to give me something random to describe.
- He said, "describe a motorbike."
- I have never owned a motorbike.
- But I did do an intensive course fifteen years ago, and now have a licence to ride bikes over 500cc.
- Ok, I'll use a 20 second snapshot of one of the rides from that course. 20 seconds will stop it turning into a narrative.
- The numbers of each sentence correspond to the artificial rule I set myself above.

First Draft

1. Remember when stunt motorcyclists used to hurl themselves off canyons, smashing bones and being pinned back together like cyborgs?

2. Sadly, it all comes back to me on day three of my intensive motorcycling course.

3. We take the slip road, scything through space and time with impossible acceleration, so much more sudden than a car, and I find myself struggling to think quickly enough as this machine lurches onward.

4. In the car park, it looked squat and fat-bellied, like an old-fashioned prop forward, yet here, in its element, it has become a muscular winger.

5. Although I am accelerating faster than any roadworthy car, this is just a lesson, and I feel the first stomach lurching of fear.

6. Ahead, Andy forgets to check his mirror.

7. Time slows as his machine joins the carriageway, inches in front of a speeding saloon, like a movie monster, bloodied teeth slashing a finger tip behind the hero.

8. Perhaps that's when I know I'll never buy a bike of my own, immersed in this river of speed.

9. Cars kiss the air as they clatter by, engines a cacophony of pistons; rubber rattling the tarmac.

10. The traffic has an undertow, and the motorbike and I must speed along it, fearful of drowning, waiting for a slowing of the current, when we can sweep across its side.

11. Surely a sign will signal left, and the sea of cars will part, and shoot me gratefully out, to spin me away from danger.

12. But no, the machine's hot throbbing is still sending vibrations through my wrists, my palms receiving the juddering signals like Morse code: S.O.S., S.O.S. on repeat.

13. The silver speedometer winks at me: wheels spinning beneath me at seventy miles an hour, and just a coat to stop my limbs being ripped off by cars or tarmac, should we slip.

14. How is this a legal pursuit?

15. I steel myself, pinning each fear down with allen keys and bolts, so that my fear won't show beneath my helmet and my cyborg head will lift up, at home in a careering universe

Stage 2 – Redrafting

Some of your sentences will work really well, and some will be clumsy or awkward.

1. Now, get rid of any bits that don't work.
2. Add in extra sentences where you think you need them.
3. Make sure your imagery works together.
4. Make sure all your sentences start with a different word. Change word order if you need to.

Redraft

1. **Remember** when stunt motorcyclists used to hurl themselves off canyons, smashing bones and being pinned back together like cyborgs?
2. **Sadly**, it all comes back to me on day three of my intensive motorcycling course.
3. **We** take the slip road, scything through space and time with impossible acceleration, so much more sudden than a car. **I** can't think. **The** machine lurches onward.
4. **In** the car park, it looked squat and fat-bellied, like an old-fashioned prop forward, yet here, in its element, it has become a muscular winger.
5. **Warp** speed kicks in before I have time to realise what I have done. **My** stomach lurches with fear.
6. **Ahead**, Andy forgets his mirror check.
7. **Time** slows as his machine joins the carriageway, inches in front of a speeding saloon, like a movie monster, bloodied teeth slashing a finger tip behind the hero.
8. **Perhaps** that's when I know I'll never buy a bike of my own, immersed in this river of speed.
9. **Cars** kiss the air as they clatter by, engines a cacophony of pistons; rubber rattling the tarmac.
10. **Traffic** has an undertow, and the motorbike and I must speed along it, fearful of drowning, waiting for a slowing of the current, when we can sweep across its side.
11. **Surely** a sign will signal an exit left, and the sea of cars will part, and shoot me gratefully out, to spin me away from danger.
12. **But** no, the machine's hot throbbing is still sending vibrations through my wrists, my palms receiving the juddering signals like Morse code: S.O.S., S.O.S. on repeat.
13. **The** silver speedometer winks at me as the bike hugs the lanes like touchlines. **Wheels** spin beneath me at seventy miles an hour, and just a coat to stop my limbs being ripped off by cars or tarmac, should we slip.
14. **How** is this a legal pursuit?
15. **I** steel myself, pinning each fear down with allen keys and bolts, so that my fear won't show beneath my helmet and my cyborg head will lift up, at home in a careering universe.

351 Words

Journeys Through a Place You Know Well

Journey Through the Park (everyone can visit a park. Do it this week!)

1. Read the description below.
2. It is a training exercise, to get you to really look at what you are seeing. It is worth trying for yourself.

- I went to the park with my phone. I filmed as I walked the dog, with a handful of seconds on each shot.
- When I got home, I put each shot together in the order of the walk - so structure took care of itself.
- Then I set a rule where I had to describe each shot in one or two sentences.
- Each description had to be constructed from these two questions:
    - What do I see?
    - What does this remind me of?
- My answers usually have to include a metaphor or simile, shown in bold below.

Autumn bustles her way into the park, calling to the strolling mothers, too young for school.
The silent bandstand longs for music, but the chatting mothers, dazed by sunlight, slip by.
The aged trees perform a guard of honour as autumn marries summer.
They send confetti in a shower of leaves. The ground is rusted gold.
A toddler smacks at the shimmering air.
The trees are stripping slowly, as autumn prepares her honeymoon.
Summer lifts a veil of sunlight, catching the lace of spider web, **ready to kiss the morning.**
Ornamental trees dazzle, blood red, rich and ripening.
Your spirits lift your gaze **to a kaleidoscope of greens.**
The park spins under your heel. A dizziness of colours, until the concrete paths break **nature's spell.**
The toddler is smacking squirrels who have fled.
A storm of leaves arrives like snowfall without winter's sting. **Now the leaves turn to dry rain.**
Amazed, you look up to a cloudless sky. **Bushes reach out to you, blood red berries in their palms.**
Shadows spring like roots at your feet, **and you are painted in silhouette in the dying leaves**.
The tall trees steal summer's generous warmth.
Squirrels also plunder the rusting ground, scampering away with gold, climbing like burglars onto rooftops, where they wait unseen.

The green trees show off their leaves. Another squirrel scurries to the sky.

An old dog plods, too tired to chase.

Young families glide by, **still in the springtime of youth.**

You notice **a tree, gashed and weeping: a delta of sap spills out.**

Sunlight or shadow? Which will win?

The old dog plods on, in an aimless circle, while the bandstand's clock ticks toward twelve.

Something is ending.

A child's picture book flutters on a park bench, commemorating the dead.

Time has cut down other giants, and centenarian trees gaze at the sawn down stump.

Ranks of benches line the route, each a life well lived or lost.

Sunshine or shadow? Which will win?

The flower beds still grow, **some unfurling flags of colour, celebrating the sun.**

The ornamental pond springs to life, and **the sky peers into its murky mirror.**

A prison riot of birds protest their innocence behind bars, free from cats and the coming winter. Are the bars better than cold and risk?

The fountain froths icing onto its wedding cake layers. It's ripples beat a shimmering circle and **a floating filigree of light.**

The park keeper's cottage is hidden in the bushes, like a character in a fairy tale. A warning of a modern plague stands at one wall.

A dead carpet of leaves sees you home.

435 Words

What to Learn From This

1. I've set it out in video shots, so you can see how it is made. It would be easy to reorganise in paragraphs. It would gain grade 9 in an exam even if it wasn't rearranged, even though there are many bits I would change or get rid of doing a second draft. For example the dog, some of the squirrels, the toddler, the question, the tree with sap …

2. The ending is easy to craft - you just return to an image from the beginning - the falling leaves. It is also easy to add in a change - the leaves are now dead, rather than associated with marriage. The idea of going 'home', guided by a 'dead carpet of leaves' also suggests a symbolic ending of death.

3. Once you have thought of an image, it is easy to keep coming back to it - look at all the wedding imagery at the beginning, and how the fountain at the end is like a wedding cake.

4. All the descriptions are built around a positive and negative contrast - death and life, spring and autumn, which builds a kind of structure.

5. The structure is just a journey - this ALWAYS works as a way to structure your description - especially if you always think about 2, 3 and 4 above.

6. Everything in bold is a metaphor.

7. This description is much more like a poem than a description in a novel, but it is still a 100% real description because poems are real texts which people read. It is not just something created for the exam.

Task

- **Find two examples of soft sounds which work well, and explain why.**
- **Find two examples of harsh sounds which work well, and explain why.**

To see what I was looking at, watch the video: *Mr Salles Description Masterclass: Writing in Pictures*

Writing Task

Remember to practise using the 3 things you noticed which were new to you.

Either

- Visit somewhere and film it in 5 second clips, as I did with the park. Write 1 or 2 descriptive sentences for each clip, using the rules I followed. Submit it.

Or

- Film that visit and make a similar video.

Or

- Take my description, edit it, change it, paragraph it, and turn it into a 350 words description you like.

Journey Through the House as Memories

Let's approach from the garden, the road less travelled. This garage, erected over a weekend from prefabricated concrete, once had an asbestos roof which fell in, scattering cancer perhaps -time will tell. The rubber membrane I added, after rebuilding it from scratch. It's as waterproof as your own skin.

Now we pass the compost heap where the trampoline used to be, and the children used to re-enact Wrestlemania. That spectator sport has been replaced by purple wildflowers – no idea what they're called, but they look like exotic eyeballs growing on giant stems.

Along here the pond used to sit, until it silted up with leaves and discarded dog toys. Not toys for discarded dogs, you understand; no, the dog himself stashed them there. I dug it up, and two sinks which past residents had buried, like memories of trauma. No bodies. Well, it's more cheerful now. A beach of white stones, which my wife calls the Zen garden, surrounds a giant hanging chair. My wife curls up in it like a womb.

The lawn, like the rest of the garden, was mud and weeds last year. Nature's not for everyone. I dug it up. I scattered seed so generously, the local birds dropped everything, and flocked to the banquet. At my arrival, they took to the trees and showed their annoyance in dollops, plummeting and splattering from the branches.

The patio is a sun trap in summer, and my son comes out to delight the neighbours, all buff and banter. But now, under the gazebo, it's the dog's territory and he marks it in the typical way. Nature, not just an acquired taste, but also an acquired smell.

Let's leave these unsavoury thoughts behind and enter the double doors. The less said about the utility room the better. The toilet used to be my library, before the iPad. A man has to hide somewhere from small, demanding children, desperate to set off into the excitement of the day.

Now the kitchen, a taste of summer brought to you in Mediterranean tiles, and lemon coloured cupboards. The centrepiece, a breakfast bar, is redundant now, but four of us used to cluster round it every meal time. I taught my daughter maths right there. The first time, she wailed, tore out clumps of her own hair and bashed her head on it, in protest, fear, and horror. She was six. I held back tears and we played with wooden blocks until the mysteries were revealed. You'd think the school might ask how we'd worked this miracle, after they had taught her three years of failure, but no.

And so, to the living room. My favourite furniture is the table, its pine top made of thick strips, dense as oak beams, and scored with rough seams. Remember when King Kong held Fay Wray in his thick palm, criss-crossed with leathery wrinkles?* No, of course you don't, it's a black and white movie. But I always wanted to reach through the screen and touch that incredible palm. Perhaps elephant skin is easier to picture. It's the massiveness, the roughness which is also gentle, which I love. Maybe the reminder of tree bark delights me, as though the table is a perfect table, yet still the essence of tree.

My mother's painting hangs on the 'accent' wall (a feature which was all the rage three years ago and, who knows, may be fashionable still). A rich burgundy wall; the painting is a bright Mediterranean town on a hilltop, where the castle has fought the church for supremacy and won. I love the way my mother has played with shape, so that all the buildings are two dimensional, while the castle and the hill are fully three dimensional and alive. In the foreground, rounded washerwomen clean their clothes. In the corner, half a poster reveals the rear end of a bull, on its way to a noble death in the ring. My mother too has died, and this is why I have allowed the patina of her nicotine to turn the brilliant scene patchy.

One day soon I'll have it professionally cleaned, and rediscover it like a lost memory.

Now, let's finish with the dog. Yes, he's sixteen now, another memory in the making I'm afraid. I know, who knew such a small body could contain so much smell!

Why This Technique Works

1. It takes almost zero planning - you just choose where to start and then plan a real route through your house.

2. Describe a memory for each place which leaps out at you. This allows you naturally to create contrast with before and after description.

3. Because it is a tour, and you are a guide, it allows you to be formal yet conversational, inviting the reader in.

4. Because you are describing real memories, you don't have to waste time thinking about what to write. Instead you can spend time thinking about the best way to describe a memory.

5. Because you are associating memories with places, your description has a double layer - the place and the memory come alive.

6. The ending is easy - you return to an image from earlier in the description which fits naturally. Here, it is the dog and his malodorous presence in my life. But I could have taken you to the front door - to the road most taken. Or to the front garden as a contrast to the back garden, or to a neighbour who used to play on the trampoline - easy to do.

Task

- Pick your favourite metaphor and explain why you think it works.
- Pick your favourite simile and explain why you think it works.
- Find an example of soft sounds which work well.
- Find an example of hard or harsh sounds which work well.
- Would it have been better with a list?

*King Kong was made in 1933 in case you are interested!

Writing Task

1. Highlight the best simile, metaphor, consonance, sibilance and contrast.

2. Write your own journey through your house and memories. 300-500 words.

3. Practise the skills you have been learning.

Seafront Journey - putting it all together

- This journey was also a real one, a walk at a seaside town. Just like the park, I simply took a series of 2-3 second videos of everything I looked at. It is called: *Mr Salles Top Grade Descriptive Writing for Q5*

- Then I turned each of these shots into a short description, including a comparison.

Some joker has spun the street signs **in a Russian roulette**, *so the town centre languishes* on the beach. A family circle their dog, hoping to be guided, but she's saying nothing, unlike the yellow coated cockle catcher, boasting next to his steaming sacks. He is mimicked by a life-sized, custard coated fisherman, posed with a wooden fish.

Ragged flags tear at the wind. The dock comes alive with metal, *clanking like a convict's chains.* The decks of fishing boats **explode with clutter:** *tangled nets like discarded hair extensions,* after a night out at sea; snakes of rubber rope sleep on the quay; *chains and rope lie in a coiled embrace*, a parody of lovers, or modern art.

Boats are docked in pairs, **secretly holding hands.** The single boats, painted a blushing red, *hug the harbour walls, like shy teenagers at the school prom.*

Local traders have converted beach huts, flickering with neon invitations to buy. Tourists in their torn jeans traipse on, past the **desperate coffee stalls and oyster bars.** *Their campervans are washed up everywhere*, like flotsam. Their dogs **survey their dominions from front seat thrones**, that come-and-get-me look in their eyes.

With the face of a giant toad, a buggy sits on the sand among **sailing boats flocked on the shore. Smaller boats lie exhausted, caught on the shingle**. Families stand at the water's edge, dreaming of escape. A flutter of birds bathe in a puddle, sending ripples to the sky.

Pebbles carpet the beach *like spat out gum: gobs of seaweed like last night's spaghetti.* **Ranks of groins guard** against *the sea's thievery.* **The middle-aged meditate on stones, and the sea's soft susurration*.** Down the hill **strides a lone warrior** in silhouette, an extra **skin of neoprene, armour plating** against the cold.

Like bare-footed Achilles*, he strides towards the sea, only to find **Scandinavian mothers, careless of the cold,** *spinning like seals* in the soft cradle of the waves.

The shore is lined with beach huts, **rows of identikit commuters crowding a platform,** *each clutching a balcony like an open laptop*. **A jogger chugs noisily down their track.**
They paint their faces in pastel shades before boarding, **but their faces still look blank, frozen in Botox.**

A garbage truck offers its best tortoise impression, while cyclists yearn to glide by.
The ice cream shops still advertise summer: **their facades are false promises**, shuttered windows, locked doors. Even the kites are flying at half-mast; **one has died in the long grass.**

Empty benches watch the horizon, one with two bouquets strapped to its sides, *like flaming torches in a Shakespeare play*. **Two dogs and a council litter picker are the only groundlings***, more interested in each other. *A lone seagull storms off like an offended critic.*

A beacon stands against the wind, wearing an empty crown. It too has lost its fire.

*susurration – a whispering, murmuring or rustling sound
*Achilles was the best and most famous Greek warrior in the Trojan War. His mother was Thetis, a sea nymph, a goddess of the sea.
*groundlings – the audience in a Shakespearian theatre who paid for the cheapest tickets. This meant they had to stand on the ground to watch the play.

478 Words

How to Think About the Description

1. Notice that there are 31 Metaphors - these are in bold.
2. And there are 11 Similes – these are in italics.

- When you watch the video, you will see that I simply filmed what I saw on a day out on the coast. Each shot lasted about 5 seconds.

- Then I wrote a description of each shot, or clip.

- This means I didn't think about structure - I just started at point A - the port, and finished at point B - by the beacon.

- The advantage of writing in this way is that I only think one description at a time - one or two sentences at most. It means my writing is packed with descriptive techniques.

Task:

1. Work out where the imagery is successfully linked as a piece of writing.

2. Work out where the imagery doesn't quite fit. I would probably get rid of the dog. And the buggy would have to change from a frog, which is fresh water, to some sea living creature - a seal, or a washed up fish with bulbous eyes - you get the idea.

3. Look at the extended metaphors. I really like the train platform one. If you know anything about Achilles, that one is pretty cool too - his mother was a sea goddess, so he would call to her by diving into the sea when he needed her. I like the dating boats, and the suggestion that they have had a drunken night.

4. Where has sound - harsh or soft - been used successfully, with consonance, assonance or sibilance?

5. Where do you like the contrast, and what would you change to make a better contrast?

Writing Task

1. Write a 300 -500 word description.

2. Practise at least 5 of the techniques I have been showing you.

3. Highlight them in your writing and provide a key.

For your writing, either:

A. Edit my description, to make it fit together better. Or

B. Film a journey anywhere near you - a shopping trip, a walk, a visit somewhere, a cycle ride, a trip though your garden or up your street. Whatever - no excuses - 5 seconds per clip. Then write a description for each clip. Or

C. Edit it as a video, and add your description into it, like mine.

Journey Through Violent Memories

- Read the two descriptions and do the task at the end.

The Abattoir

The killings always happened in bright sunlight. The smell of burning hair brings the first killings straight back to me, and I am five again, thirsty in the hot sun – all of us at break time queueing at the well. No running water.

Just down the hill, in a hollow, **squatted** an open shell of a building: whitewashed walls **splashed** with blood.

Once a month, the **snuffling** pigs **ambled** up the path, to the pen. They gathered nonchalantly. Then the show started. First, a hook like a giant question mark was **stabbed** through a snout. The **disbelieving** pig was **pulled**, **squealing** in shock, and just as suddenly, three shirtless men lifted it. The hook fitted onto a rail above head height. Below, a bucket, for the blood. The screaming pig **hung** from its snout, legs **kicking** at the empty air.

Yes, we children **watched** it all, **perched** on the wall above the hollow. The teachers at The Hippy School were elsewhere (it was their break time after all).

Like pirates **boarding** a ship, the men **set-to** with blade and flame. A neck was **slit**, and blood **burned** out in a lava flow. The **watching** pigs **understood** and began to **scream**. We **ignored** them.

Once dead and drained, the carcasses were **slapped** on a slab and a blowtorch **skimmed** the skin– hair **flared**, flaming like sudden sparklers, and the smell **hit** our throats.

The men **laughed** and **took** the time **to notice** us. Like circus clowns, they **picked** up buckets and **pretended to splash** us. We **screamed, stumbled** backwards, and **returned** for more. Suddenly, the blood was **released**; fountains of red **reached** towards us with wet fingers, then **slapped** the white walls with colour, beneath our **hanging** feet.

Later, **queueing** at the well, a boy tried to **push** in front of me. I **punched** his face. He fell backwards onto limestone and lay there like a corpse.

317 Words

Fishing

On the beach of my childhood, the fishermen were brutal. Once, we marvelled as they tossed dynamite overboard and the dead rose, belly-up to the surface, bone-white against the blue sea.

To kill an octopus took bravery. **Thrust** a fist into a crack, and wait for the electrified tentacles to take hold. Swim to the surface. **Turn** its head inside out, like a pocket, **to trap** in the squirting ink. The panicked tentacles release. **Grab** some and swing it like a mace, dashing its rubbery head on the rocks. **Repeat** until dead.

The summer when I was eight, I dreamed of spearfishing. I washed up for 'pesetas'– months in my parents' bar: hours and hours, dreaming of the clear blue waters, the firework coloured fish, snake-like eels and carpet-sized manta rays.

My heart burst with pride, as I strode out that first sunlit morning, spear gun cradled like a bomb. Mask, snorkel, flippers – already an expert swimmer, I slid into the sea.

The silent burst of colours throbbed with life. Each fish I hoped to hunt swum brilliantly past, and my heart sang with the thrill. Yet my fingers would not fire. My eyes would not take aim.

Astonished, I returned home, my prize spear gun stowed like a secret, beneath my startled bed.

215 Words

What to learn from these descriptions:

1. Start with a crisis.

2. Make horrible things happen to good people.

3. As so often, start with a contrast. The ending is also a contrast. Contrast is the king and queen of good writing

4. Use colour to symbolise ideas.

5. Make your similes unusual – in a class of 30, you don't want anyone using the same simile.

6. Start each sentence in a different way.

7. Concentrate on your verbs. They are the most important words in your story. I've put some of them in bold. Notice how a violent verb often appears near an ordinary, emotionless one. Contrast is king.

8. Starting sentences with imperative verbs, as I do when killing an octopus, creates both a sense of urgency and a lack of emotion – they are like instructions. **This is a useful contrast, where the narrator or character refuses to be emotional about things which we should be emotional about.**

9. Use adjectives in pairs, sometimes hyphenated.

10. Play with the soundscape of your sentences. Alliterative words don't have to be next to each other. Look at how much alliteration sneaks in this way. Notice how many of the verbs start with the same sound.

11. Enjoy sibilance, it either creates a sinister atmosphere, or silence and peace. This is really useful, as this contradiction creates contrast.

Writing Task

1. Think of times when you have witnessed or been a part of violence, or have suffered pain, broken bones, scars, etc.

2. Jot down ideas about each one till you get a feel for which ones form the deepest memories, or gives you most to describe.

3. Write a description of those memories using some or all of the techniques:

    - You have been studying though the course in this guide
    - Or focus on some key ones from this section

4. Write a 300 - 500 word description and submit it to your teacher.

Journey Through a Beach

Adapted from Ulysses, by James Joyce

His feet marched in a sudden proud rhythm over the sand furrows, along by the boulders of the south wall, **piled stone mammoth skulls**. Gold light on the sea, on sand, glinting on the slender trees, the lemon houses.

He came nearer the edge of the sea and **wet sand slapped his boots**. The **new air greeted him, a little too wildly**. He stood suddenly, his feet beginning to sink slowly in the quaking soil.

The domed tower gazed coldly back at him. Shafts of light and shadow moved across the beach. Blue dusk, nightfall, a deep blue night was coming.

He lifted his feet up from the suck and turned back by the wall of boulders. **The flood of tide felt as though it was following him**, so he clambered over the dune and sedge and weeds, then sat on a stool of rock, resting. A smell caused him to turn his head.

A bloated carcass of a dog lay lolled on seaweed, beneath the gunwale of a boat, sunk in sand. And now a sound and movement made him look up.

A quick, live dog, grew into sight, running across the sweep of sand, in a line towards him. Was he going to attack?

From farther away, two figures walked shoreward across from the rushing tide till they tucked themselves safely among the bulrushes. The dog ran back towards them, barking.

He ambled about a bank of dwindling sand, trotting, sniffing on all sides. Looking for something **lost in a past life.** Suddenly he made off *like a bounding hare*, ears flung back, chasing the shadow of a low-skimming gull. The man's shrieked whistle struck his limp ears. He turned, bounded back, came nearer, trotted on twinkling legs. At **the lace fringe of the tide** he halted with stiff forelegs and seaward-pointed ears. His snout lifted, barked at the waves *like herds of seahorses*, then noticed the cocklepickers.

The dog yelped, running to them, reared up and pawed them, dropping on all fours, again reared up at them, fawning. He kept by them as they came towards the drier sand, **a rag of wolf's tongue** panting red from his jaws. His speckled body ambled ahead of them and then loped off at **a calf's gallop**.

The carcass lay on his path. He stopped, sniffed, stalked round it, his brother dog, nosing closer, went round it again, sniffling rapidly like a dog all over the dead dog's bedraggled body.

"Fenton! Out of that, you mongrel!"

The cry brought him skulking back to his master and a blunt, barefoot kick sent him unscathed across a spit of sand, crouched in flight. He slunk back in a curve. Along by the edge of the wall he lolloped, dawdled, smelt a rock and from under a cocked hindleg pissed against it. He trotted forward and, lifting again his hindleg, pissed quick short bursts at an unsmelt rock. Simple pleasures. His hind paws then **scattered** the sand: his forepaws **dabbled** and **delved**. Something he **buried** there. He **rooted** in the sand, **dabbling, delving** and **stopped** to **listen** to the air, **scraped** up the sand again with a fury of his claws, then **ceased**, **standing** like a vicar presiding over a burial, **vulturing** the dead.

541 Words

Tasks

1. Make a list of all the verbs
2. Use these verbs in a piece of writing of your own on a similar topic or (if you are really creative, on a totally different topic).

What Else You Should Take Away From This

1. Look at the structure - following the dog as a journey
2. How it begins with an image of death, and ends with an image of death
3. How metaphor works
4. How metaphors outnumber similes
5. Where he uses sibilance, and how this fits the description
6. Where he uses harsh sounds, and how this fits the description
7. How verbs are often listed in threes

What you should have learned:

Adapted from Ulysses, by James Joyce

His feet marched in a sudden proud rhythm over the sand furrows, along by the boulders of the south wall, **piled stone mammoth skulls**. Gold light on the sea, on sand, glinting on the slender trees, the lemon houses.

- The stones like mammoth skulls foreshadow the discovery of the dead dog.
- This is echoed by the semantic field of military life, where his feet "marched" to a "rhythm", just like a soldier.

He came nearer the edge of the sea and **wet sand slapped his boots**. The **new air greeted him, a little too wildly**. He stood suddenly, his feet beginning to sink slowly in the quaking soil.

- These metaphors show that nature is threatening, potentially dangerous. Again, this foreshadows the death of the dog, presumably from drowning.

The domed tower gazed coldly back at him. Shafts of light and shadow moved across the beach. Blue dusk, nightfall, a deep blue night was coming.

- This metaphor helps us picture a tower which is falling in to disrepair. But 'doomed' also invites us to think of death.

He lifted his feet up from the suck and turned back by the wall of boulders. *__The flood of tide felt as though it was following him__*, so he clambered over the dune and **sedge and weeds, then sat on a stool of rock, resting. A smell caused** him to turn his head.

- This simile personifies the sea as dangerous, again foreshadowing the death of the drowned dog. It also uses fricative alliteration to emphasise the danger of the tide.
- This sinister mood is also built through the sibilance in **sedge, weeds, sat, stool, resting, smell, caused**.

A bloated carcass of a dog lay lolled on seaweed, beneath the gunwale of a boat, sunk in sand. And now a sound and movement made him look up.

A quick, live dog, grew into sight, running across the sweep of sand, in a line towards him. Was he going to attack?

- Joyce couldn't make the contrast any more obvious! The dead dog contrasted to the live one.

From farther away, two figures walked shoreward across from the rushing tide till they tucked themselves safely among the bulrushes. The dog ran back towards them, barking.

He ambled about a bank of dwindling sand, trotting, sniffing on all sides. Looking for something **lost in a past life.** Suddenly he made off ***like a bounding hare***, ears flung back, chasing the shadow of a low-skimming gull. The man's shrieked whistle struck his limp ears. He turned, bounded back, came nearer, **trotted on twinkling** legs.

- This astonishing description helps us see all dogs differently. The metaphor of a dog looking for "something lost in a past life" is a brilliant description of a dog following a scent which humans can't smell. Scents are laid down long in the past - a dog reads history through layers of scent.
- The suddenness of the change in the dog's behaviour is captured with the simile of the dog "like a bounding hare".
- The alliteration of "trotted on twinkling legs" is fantastic. The dog is now like a horse, trotting, but also like the play of light on water, or light and shadow, with "twinkling". The change from "hare" to horse suggests that the dog is mercurial, a kind of shapeshifter, always moving, always changing. This is a really vivid way of showing the dog's changing mood and actions on the beach.

At **the lace fringe of the tide** he halted with stiff forelegs and seaward-pointed ears. His snout lifted, barked at the waves ***like herds of seahorses***, then noticed the cocklepickers.

- The sea is wearing a dress with a "lace fringe", which is a metaphor for the white froth of the tide on the shore. This is contrasts with the dog, whose movement is suddenly stopped.
- The simile "like herds of seahorses" doesn't just describe the movement of the waves, but also hints at their dangerous power, linking us back to the dead dog.

The dog yelped, running to them, reared up and pawed them, dropping on all fours, again reared up at them, fawning. He kept by them as they came towards the drier sand, **a rag of wolf's tongue** panting red from his jaws. His speckled body ambled ahead of them and then loped off at **a calf's gallop**.

- These metaphors again present the dog as a shape-shifter, and again this is linked to the dog's movements.

- The tongue as a "rag" changes his threatening genetic link to the "wolf" to something harmless, but also discarded. We get the idea that the dog may not be well cared for, which is echoed by the lack of attention he gets from the cockle pickers.

The carcass lay on his path. He stopped, sniffed, stalked round it, his brother dog, nosing closer, went round it again, sniffling rapidly like a dog all over the dead dog's bedraggled body.

- The alliteration of b's and d's is percussive, it has a threatening rhythm. This fits the mood of the dog's discovery not just of a dead dog, but a dog which is similar to himself, like a "brother".

"Fenton! Out of that, you mongrel!"

The cry brought him skulking back to his master and a blunt, barefoot kick **sent him unscathed across a spit of sand**, crouched in flight. He slunk back in a curve. Along by the edge of the wall he lolloped, dawdled, smelt a rock and from under a cocked hindleg pissed against it.

- The owner's casual cruelty is emphasised through this repeated alliteration of b's and d's.
- The sibilance of "**sent him unscathed across a spit of sand**" feels sinister and matches the owner's cruelty.

He trotted forward and, lifting again his hindleg, pissed quick short bursts at an unsmelt rock. Simple pleasures. His hind paws then **scattered** the sand: his forepaws **dabbled** and **delved**. Something he **buried** there. He **rooted** in the sand, **dabbling, delving** and **stopped** to **listen** to the air, **scraped** up the sand again with a fury of his claws, then **ceased, standing *like a vicar presiding over a burial*, vulturing** the dead.

- Look at how many verbs are crammed into this description, all emphasising the dog's constant movement.

- The simile "*like a vicar presiding over a burial*" makes the scene at once serious and comic. This sense of unease is added to by the made-up verb "vulturing", which suggests that the dog might be quite happy to eat the corpse.

- The scene takes place in Ireland, in 1920, where Catholic belief would have been very strong. It was particularly strong as they were fighting The Irish War of Independence at the time.

- The simile also asks the reader to think of the vicar as a vulture, profiting from the death of the Irish. Catholics have priests, not vicars. So comparing the dog to a vicar is also an attack on the English. After lots of violence, the English retreated to Northern Ireland, which was mostly Protestant. The 'partition' of Ireland into two countries happened very soon after publication, in May 1921.

A Journey Through the Seasons: Describe the same scene in different seasons.

Mountains make you happy. **Their protective ring seems to reach up into the sky and pull the sky towards you**. It is impossible not to breathe. Where you absorb diesel and dust through your pores in the city, in the mountains' **summer air your lungs fill with sky**. It isn't only the clean taste which **cleanses you from the inside, but the texture of sky**. The thinner air forces your lungs open and your body remembers what your body is for, expanding at the rib cage, filling space as though it belongs here.

The sun, hot in the valley, invites your mind to soar upwards, and you do not resist. To climb is to enter a new world, where the sun grows brighter as the temperature drops. Paths are lined with wildflowers, every twenty minutes of determined ascent a new ecosystem blazes in different colours and shapes. **The mountain opens to you in bright invitation**, past the ski lift station, past the exhausted, sun-dazed ramblers, past the **paragliders launching themselves on thermal hopes**, past the barren scree above the treeline until you summit, exhausted hours later, dripping by the ice wall. Tourists arrive by gondola, sight-seers with picnics come to visit **the world's penthouse**. You do not sneer, but rejoice on the terrace with chilled water and colder beer.

Join me now in winter. **The same sun invites you, but much more eagerly**. Snow **has flattened its soft mattress**, its surface taut with a sheet of brilliant white. Its diamond light hints at the hardness of morning, where **night's touch has chilled the flakes to crystal**. On the chairlift, your snowboard twitches beneath you, suspended from one foot, as you ride snow-wards, upwards. The burr of the cable wire cranks gently and hums as **you drink in the view**, savouring the anticipation, knowing that you will be launched off, balancing on one foot, a picture of cool or ridicule, depending on how you control the slide off the chair.

The summit is not even half way up the full height of the next peak, **where the powder waits. The piste hurries you downward**, sawing beneath your board as though trying to sever the time between now, and the ascent on the next lift. Up there, plump and deep above the treeline, and plumper still in the shade of the trees, **huge dumps of snow spring down the mountain slopes.**

There will be bowls, and gullies, jumps and slopes, treeline slaloms for you to carve through. Your board will float, and **the soft snow will billow, with whispers**, with **rushing fingers urging you faster**, to bank and turn, to leap and bury yourself in landings that spring you waist deep before propelling you upwards, downwards, onwards, go, go, go, while your aching legs can stand it, **till your thighs burn** and you stop to scream your delight.

The silent valley soaks up your excitement and you gaze at the sky.

You cannot speak.

Task

1. Go through and find sentences with listed verbs. These are packed with action, which is a great descriptive technique.

2. Find where patterns are repeated. These give your sentences a rhythm.

3. Find sentences which use lists. These overload the description with lots of layers.

4. Notice how separating the description into two seasons automatically produces contrast. The second season will be the one you prefer.

5. Notice how many sentences are constructed around a contrast.

6. Writing in the second person invites the reader more immediately into your description.

7. Notice that each season is also presented as a journey in the mountains.

8. Notice that there are no similes, because metaphor is nearly always more powerful. These are highlighted.

9. Pick your top 5 verbs - the ones you think help the reader picture the scene best.

10. Notice there is only one adverb - because adverbs slow down action.

11. Find three sentences where the sound of words is important. Is it sibilance, assonance or consonance which you are good at noticing?

Writing Task

- Write a description of the same place in two seasons.

- Make each description a journey through the place - (think of places which are easy to travel through - the mountains were easy for me - you will have other places).

- Write 300-500 words

Journeys Through the Eyes of a Persona

Journey Through Close Up

Read the short story below. It will show you how long description can be used in real writing, rather than just for the exam:

The Fly, by Katherine Mansfield

'Y'are very snug in here,' piped old Mr. Woodifield, and peered out of the great, green-leather armchair by his friend the boss's desk as a baby peers out of its pram. His talk was over; it was time for him to be off. But he did not want to go. Since he had retired, since his…stroke, the wife and the girls kept him boxed up in the house every day of the week except Tuesday. On Tuesday he was dressed and brushed and allowed to cut back to the City for the day. Though what he did there the wife and girls couldn't imagine. Made a nuisance of himself to his friends, they supposed…Well, perhaps so. All the same, we cling to our last pleasures as the tree clings to its last leaves. So there sat old Woodifield, smoking a cigar and staring almost greedily at the boss, who rolled in his office chair, stout, rosy, five years older than he, and still going strong, still at the helm. It did one good to see him.

Wistfully, admiringly, the old voice added, 'It's snug in here, upon my word!'

'Yes, it's comfortable enough,' agreed the boss, and he flipped the Financial Times with a paper-knife. As a matter of fact he was proud of his room; he liked to have it admired, especially by old Woodifield. It gave him a feeling of deep, solid satisfaction to be planted there in the midst of it in full view of that frail old figure in the muffler.

'I've had it done up lately,' he explained, as he had explained for the past how many weeks.

'New carpet,' and he pointed to the bright red carpet with a pattern of large white rings. 'New furniture,' and he nodded towards the massive bookcase and the table with legs like twisted treacle. 'Electric heating!' He waved almost exultantly towards the five transparent, pearly sausages glowing so softly in the tilted copper pan.

But he did not draw old Woodifield's attention to the photograph over the table of a grave-looking boy in uniform standing in one of those spectral photographers' parks with photographers' storm-clouds behind him. It was not new. It had been there for over six years.

'There was something I wanted to tell you,' said old Woodifield, and his eyes grew dim remembering. 'Now what was it? I had it in my mind when I started out this morning.' His hands began to tremble, and patches of red showed above his beard.

Poor old chap, he's on his last pins, thought the boss. And, feeling kindly, he winked at the old man, and said jokingly,

'I tell you what. I've got a little drop of something here that'll do you good before you go out into the cold again. It's beautiful stuff. It wouldn't hurt a child.' He took a key off his watch-chain, unlocked a cupboard below his desk, and drew forth a dark, squat bottle. 'That's the medicine,' said he. 'And the man from whom I got it told me on the strict Q.T. it came from the cellars at Windsor Castle.'

Old Woodifield's mouth fell open at the sight. He couldn't have looked more surprised if the boss had produced a rabbit.

'It's whisky, ain't it?' he piped feebly.

The boss turned the bottle and lovingly showed him the label. Whisky it was.

'D'you know,' said he, peering up at the boss wonderingly, 'they won't let me touch it at home.' And he looked as though he was going to cry.

'Ah, that's where we know a bit more than the ladies,' cried the boss, swooping across for two tumblers that stood on the table with the water-bottle, and pouring a generous finger into each. 'Drink it down. It'll do you good. And don't put any water with it. It's sacrilege to tamper with stuff like this. Ah!' He tossed off his, pulled out his handkerchief, hastily wiped his moustaches, and cocked an eye at old Woodifield, who was rolling his in his chaps.

The old man swallowed, was silent a moment, and then said faintly, 'It's nutty!'

But it warmed him; as it crept into his chill old brain he remembered.

'That was it,' he said, heaving himself out of his chair.

'I thought you'd like to know. The girls were in Belgium last week having a look at poor Reggie's grave, and they happened to come across your boy's. They're quite near each other, it seems.'

Old Woodifield paused, but the boss made no reply. Only a quiver in his eyelids showed that he heard.

'The girls were delighted with the way the place is kept,' piped the old voice. 'Beautifully looked after. Couldn't be better if they were at home. You've not been across, have yer?'

'No, no!' For various reasons the boss had not been across.

'There's miles of it,' quavered old Woodifield, 'and it's all as neat as a garden. Flowers growing on all the graves. Nice broad paths.' It was plain from his voice how much he liked a nice broad path.

The pause came again. Then the old man brightened wonderfully.

'D'you know what the hotel made the girls pay for a pot of jam?' he piped. 'Ten francs! Robbery, I call it. It was a little pot, so Gertrude says, no bigger than a half-crown. And she hadn't taken more than a spoonful when they charged her ten francs. Gertrude brought the pot away with her to teach 'em a lesson. Quite right, too; it's trading on our feelings. They think because we're over there having a look round we're ready to pay anything. That's what it is.' And he turned towards the door.

'Quite right, quite right!' cried the boss, though what was quite right he hadn't the least idea. He came round by his desk, followed the shuffling footsteps to the door, and saw the old fellow out. Woodifield was gone.

For a long moment the boss stayed, staring at nothing, while the grey-haired office messenger, watching him, dodged in and out of his cubby-hole like a dog that expects to be taken for a run. Then: 'I'll see nobody for half an hour, Macey,' said the boss. 'Understand! Nobody at all.'

'Very good, sir.'

The door shut, the firm heavy steps recrossed the bright carpet, the fat body plumped down in the spring chair, and leaning forward, the boss covered his face with his hands. He wanted, he intended, he had arranged to weep...

It had been a terrible shock to him when old Woodifield sprang that remark upon him about the boy's grave. It was exactly as though the earth had opened and he had seen the boy lying there with Woodifield's girls staring down at him. For it was strange. Although over six years had passed away, the boss never thought of the boy except as lying unchanged, unblemished in his uniform, asleep for ever. 'My son!' groaned the boss. But no tears came yet. In the past, in the first months and even years after the boy's death, he had only to say those words to be overcome by such grief that nothing short of a violent fit of weeping could relieve him. Time, he had declared then, he had told everybody, could make no difference. Other men perhaps might recover, might live their loss down, but not he. How was it possible! His boy was an only son. Ever since his birth the boss had worked at building up this business for him; it had no other meaning if it was not for the boy. Life itself had come to have no other meaning. How on earth could he have slaved, denied himself, kept going all those years without the promise for ever before him of the boy's stepping into his shoes and carrying on where he left off?

And that promise had been so near being fulfilled. The boy had been in the office learning the ropes for a year before the war. Every morning they had started off together; they had come back by the same train. And what congratulations he had received as the boy's father! No wonder; he had taken to it marvellously. As to his popularity with the staff, every man jack of them down to old Macey couldn't make enough of the boy. And he wasn't in the least spoilt. No, he was just his bright natural self, with the right word for everybody, with that boyish look and his habit of saying, 'Simply splendid!'

But all that was over and done with as though it never had been. The day had come when Macey had handed him the telegram that brought the whole place crashing about his head. 'Deeply regret to inform you ...' And he had left the office a broken man, with his life in ruins.

Six years ago, six years.... How quickly time passed! It might have happened yesterday. The boss took his hands from his face; he was puzzled. Something seemed to be wrong with him. He wasn't feeling as he wanted to feel. He decided to get up and have a look at the boy's photograph. But it wasn't a favourite photograph of his; the expression was unnatural. It was cold, even stern-looking. The boy had never looked like that.

At that moment the boss noticed that a fly had fallen into his broad inkpot, and was trying feebly but desperately to clamber out again. Help! Help! said those struggling legs. But the sides of the inkpot were wet and slippery; it fell back again and began to swim. The boss took up a pen, picked the fly out of the ink, and shook it on to a piece of blotting-paper. For a fraction of a second it lay still on the dark patch that oozed round it. Then the front legs waved, took hold, and, pulling its small, sodden body up, it began the immense task of cleaning the ink from its wings. Over and under, over and under, went a leg along a wing as the stone goes over and under the scythe. Then there was a pause, while the fly, seeming to stand on the tips of its toes, tried to expand first one wing and then the other. It succeeded at last, and, sitting down, it began, like a minute cat, to clean its face. Now one could imagine that the little front legs rubbed against each other lightly, joyfully. The horrible danger was over; it had escaped; it was ready for life again.

But just then the boss had an idea. He plunged his pen back into the ink, leaned his thick wrist on the blotting-paper, and as the fly tried its wings down came a great heavy blot. What would it make of that! What indeed! The little beggar seemed absolutely cowed, stunned, and afraid to move because of what would happen next. But then, as if painfully, it dragged itself forward. The front legs waved, caught hold, and, more slowly this time, the task began from the beginning.

He's a plucky little devil, thought the boss, and he felt a real admiration for the fly's courage. That was the way to tackle things; that was the right spirit. Never say die; it was only a question of... But the fly had again finished its laborious task, and the boss had just time to refill his pen, to shake fair and square on the new-cleaned body yet another dark drop. What about it this time? A painful moment of suspense followed. But behold, the front legs were again waving; the boss felt a rush of relief. He leaned over the fly and said to it tenderly, 'You artful little b...' And he actually had the brilliant notion of breathing on it to help the drying process. All the same, there was something timid and weak about its efforts now, and the boss decided that this time should be the last, as he dipped the pen deep into the inkpot.

It was. The last blot fell on the soaked blotting-paper, and the draggled fly lay in it and did not stir. The back legs were stuck to the body; the front legs were not to be seen.

'Come on,' said the boss. 'Look sharp!' And he stirred it with his pen in vain. Nothing happened or was likely to happen. The fly was dead.

(519 Word description in italics)

The boss lifted the corpse on the end of the paper-knife and flung it into the waste-paper basket. But such a grinding feeling of wretchedness seized him that he felt positively frightened. He started forward and pressed the bell for Macey.

'Bring me some fresh blotting-paper,' he said sternly, 'and look sharp about it.' And while the old dog padded away he fell to wondering what it was he had been thinking about before. What was it? It was... He took out his handkerchief and passed it inside his collar. For the life of him he could not remember.

What to Learn From This Description

1. Slow down time to focus on one significant detail.
2. Good description should fit into a story.
3. The description works best if it is described from a persona's perspective.

Find the examples from the bullet points in the paragraph above them.

At that moment the boss noticed that a fly had fallen into his broad inkpot, and was trying feebly but desperately to clamber out again. Help! Help! said those struggling legs. But the sides of the inkpot were wet and slippery; it fell back again and began to swim.

- adverbs slow down time
- adjectives in pairs
- power of verbs

The boss took up a pen, picked the fly out of the ink, and shook it on to a piece of blotting-paper. For a fraction of a second it lay still on the dark patch that oozed round it. Then the front legs waved, took hold, and, pulling its small, sodden body up, it began the immense task of cleaning the ink from its wings. Over and under, over and under, went a leg along a wing as the stone goes over and under the scythe. Then there was a pause, while the fly, seeming to stand on the tips of its toes, tried to expand first one wing and then the other. It succeeded at last, and, sitting down, it began, like a minute cat, to clean its face. Now one could imagine that the little front legs rubbed against each other lightly, joyfully. The horrible danger was over; it had escaped; it was ready for life again.

- adverbs slow down time
- adjectives in pairs
- power of verbs
- simile

But just then the boss had an idea. He plunged his pen back into the ink, leaned his thick wrist on the blotting-paper, and as the fly tried its wings down came a great heavy blot. What would it make of that! What indeed! The little beggar seemed absolutely cowed, stunned, and afraid to move because of what would happen next. But then, as if painfully, it dragged itself forward. The front legs waved, caught hold, and, more slowly this time, the task began from the beginning.

- adverbs slow down time
- adjectives in pairs
- power of verbs

He's a plucky little devil, thought the boss, and he felt a real admiration for the fly's courage. That was the way to tackle things; that was the right spirit. Never say die; it was only a question of... But the fly had again finished its laborious task, and the boss had just time to refill his pen, to shake fair and square on the new-cleaned body yet another dark drop. What about it this time? A painful moment of suspense followed. But behold, the front legs were again waving; the boss felt a rush of relief. He leaned over the fly and said to it tenderly, 'You artful little b...' And he actually had the brilliant notion of breathing on it to help the drying process. All the same, there was something timid and weak about its efforts now, and the boss decided that this time should be the last, as he dipped the pen deep into the inkpot.

- Contrast
- The persona's voice

It was. The last blot fell on the soaked blotting-paper, and the draggled fly lay in it and did not stir. The back legs were stuck to the body; the front legs were not to be seen. 'Come on,' said the boss. 'Look sharp!' And he stirred it with his pen in vain. Nothing happened or was likely to happen. The fly was dead.

- short sentences for effect

Now Let's Look at the Contrast

- Work out how the contrast works

At that moment the boss noticed that a fly had fallen into his broad inkpot, and was trying feebly but desperately to clamber out again. Help! Help! said those struggling legs. But the sides of the inkpot were wet and slippery; it fell back again and began to swim.
The boss took up a pen, picked the fly out of the ink, and shook it on to a piece of **blotting-paper**. For a fraction of a second it lay **still** on the **dark patch that oozed** round it. Then the front legs **waved, took hold, and, pulling** its **small**, sodden **body** up, it began the **immense task** of cleaning the ink from its wings. Over and under, over and under, went a leg along a wing as the stone goes over and under the scythe. Then there was a pause, while the **fly**, seeming to stand on the tips of its toes, tried to expand first one wing and then the other. It succeeded at last, and, sitting down, it began, like a minute **cat**, to clean its face. Now one could imagine that the little front legs rubbed against each other lightly, joyfully. The horrible **danger** was over; it had **escaped**; it was ready for life again.
But just then the boss had an idea. He plunged his pen back into the ink, leaned his **thick** wrist on the blotting-paper, and as the fly tried its wings down came a **great heavy blot**. What would it make of that! What indeed! The little beggar seemed absolutely cowed, stunned, and afraid to move because of what would happen next. But then, as if painfully, it dragged itself forward. The front legs waved, caught hold, and, more slowly this time, the task began from the beginning.

- Contrast uses irony - the cat has nine lives, contrasted to the four of the fly

He's a plucky little devil, thought the boss, and he felt a real admiration for the fly's courage. That was the way to tackle things; that was the right spirit. **Never say die**; it was only a question of... But the fly had again finished its laborious task, and the boss had just time to refill his pen, to shake **fair and square** on the new-cleaned body yet another dark drop. What about it this time? **A painful moment** of suspense followed. But behold, the front legs were again waving; the boss felt **a rush of relief**. He leaned over the fly and **said to it**

tenderly, 'You artful little b...' And he actually had the brilliant notion of **breathing on it to help the drying process**. All the same, there was something timid and weak about its efforts now, and **the boss decided that this time should be the last**, as he dipped the pen deep into the inkpot.

It was. The last blot fell on the soaked blotting-paper, and the draggled fly lay in it and did not stir. The back legs were stuck to the body; the front legs were not to be seen.

'Come on,' said the boss. 'Look sharp!' And he stirred it with his pen in vain. Nothing happened or was likely to happen. The fly was dead.

Writing Task

- Pick something small. An insect caught in a spider's web, a bee in a flower, a bird at a feeder, a cat in a patch of sun, two dogs meeting, ducks being fed, a toddler learning to ride a bike...

- Then introduce a crisis, like the fly experienced.

- Write the description in 300-500 words.

Journey: Dog's Eye View

Metaphors and similes are in bold:

Let's start with the mat arrangements. They look kind, piled one on top of the other for my aching bones, sure, but I tell you any mutt with half a brain can see I need some stability, **not a mat that skates across their polished floorboards. One minute a carpet, the next a raft spinning towards rapids.**

- What is the effect of these metaphors in understanding the dog?

Yes, that's them, the geniuses reclining on the couch there, **bathed in the blue light** of their laptops while Netflix plays on the big screen: background noise. If I hear another 'it's my duty, Philip', I'll jump through the screen and clamp my remaining teeth around one of those fluffy Corgi necks.

- Notice that having a persona allows you to be really sarcastic. It's fun to write from this point of view.

Anyway, my blue-faced owners have grown harder to train. Look at them, tapping away **like raindrops** on their keyboards, while I struggle to stand. Once I'm up, I make sure to tip-tap on the floor with all 16 claws, **a monsoon answering their gentle shower**. It's satirical, see? Eventually one of them will get up, waddle over to the door and let me out, so they won't have to listen to me any more.

- Linking your imagery (here the simile and the metaphor) makes the writing feel much more complete.
- Notice the verb choice of "waddle" which shows the dog's disgust at his owners.

It's the lights that kill me: everywhere I turn, there's a glow. Three lamps blaze on various surfaces, a fat stump of a candle flames by the fireplace, while at the hearth, some monstrous plastic bush, with twenty orange bulbs **like blown glass** thrusts itself into the room. And then, the Christmas tree, a travesty in plastic, smothered in baubles and fairy lights. I shut my eyes, and my retinas are still assaulted **with the Milky Way spinning away inside my eyelids**.

- There's Dickens' power of the list again.
- If you've seen a picture of the Milky Way galaxy, you'll remember it is in the shape of a spiral. This works really well with "spinning". The idea of stars matches the image of what happens when you shut your eyes after looking at bright lights.

I'd mark my territory on this pale Nordic imitation with a pee, but the arthritis won't let me cock my leg, and if I get the angle of the spray wrong any one of those winking lights might electrocute me. Then there's **the skating rink of the floorboards** to navigate and, I think I mentioned the full horror of this before, the damned tree is plastic: urine resistant.

- The simile of the 'skating rink' gives us a clear picture of how unsteady the dog is on the polished floorboards. But skating rink also links well with winter and Christmas.

On the bright side, I do get pride of place by the radiator, so I can sleep soundly. Sometimes I wake myself up running in a dream, to find my paws are scampering **on its metal ridges**

like a skiffle board. She, the short one who deposits four pairs of glasses all around the living room **like boobytraps**, is quite the musician. It only takes six notes of a song as the background music to a film to set her off. I'm sure there is more than a hint of wolf in her lupine wailing. I try to join in. I keep expecting her to recognise 'Danny Boy' as I scratch it out on the radiator's skiffle, but no. Not a single note. **Pearls before swine.***

- If you don't know what a skiffle board is, Google.
- The simile of 'boobytraps' reveals that the female owner is dangerous and possibly stupid, risking damage to all her glasses.

*Jesus told his disciples "Do not give what is holy to the dogs; nor cast your pearls before swine", in the Book of Matthew 7:6. The pig was an unclean animals which Jews were forbidden to eat. In popular language, the phrase is a warning not to give things you value to people who don't deserve it (not a very Christian message!)

What You Should Take Away From This

1. The advantages of having a persona, so description develops the scene and character at the same time.

2. An unusual perspective, which just helps you and your reader see things differently and originally.

3. Using allusions which you think the reader in 20 years' time will still understand. Did you spot 'The Crown' from Netflix? Even if the show is not remembered then, the Queen's addiction to Corgis will be a part of history.

4. As always, the verbs do so much of the work.

5. Metaphor is superior to simile, as the reader adds 2+2.

Write Your Own Journey Through the House

- Pick the persona of a pet which will move through your house.
- Or an invader, like a mouse, rat or spider.
- Give it a distinctive voice - here the dog felt superior in intelligence. Your pet or invader can also be intelligent, or sneaky, or disgusting - pick a point of view which will be interesting for you to describe in.

A Grandfather's Journey Round the Home

Ah, you're here. Welcome, come in. Mind the coat stand, covered as it is in **an explosion of coats, hats, windbreakers**, the **shed skin** of too many children and grandchildren. Mind the shoes, oops, there they go, **skittering like mice in a cheese factory**. Yes, I suppose carpet would have been a better choice for the hallway, something in burgundy perhaps, but instead, as you see, we have laminated Ash. Not burnt trees, you understand, just the dead kind. Slippery, but easy to clean.

- Notice that this works like one side of conversation.
- The choice of imagery makes the persona seem unpleasant (which is always more fun to write, and more interesting for the examiner to read).

When the **ankle-biters** aren't visiting, of course, we have the dogs. **Bundles of fun**, fluff and, sadly, filth. The laminate is easy to mop, and if you get the water temperature just right, it lasts long enough to skate on. I like the fun of skittling along and aiming the poodles at grand-children, **like bowling balls**.

- The fricative alliteration of fun, fluff and filth gives us a sense of disgust.

Now we come to the living room. The Christmas tree is up already, true. It's the lights**, a mini universe** scattered around Norwegian pine, that draw you in, **like wise men to the manger**. Chocolates hidden everywhere, **like gossip**, **desperate to find the right tongue**!

- One metaphor and two similes which, I hope, are all original.

Two toilet roll snowmen (made when my daughter was five) still take pride of place. The tree is a memory palace of decorations bought to mark important events, with baubles everywhere **like a Russian church**. You know, with the onion shaped domes.

- These are all real decorations on our Christmas tree. Describing somewhere you know well makes the task much easier.
- The Russian church domes perfectly describe the shape of the baubles, but so would onions or domes. The church reference works even better, because this is Christmas.

Well, it's not all nostalgia. The white cupboards newly minted in the alcoves, the photo albums parading either side of the gorilla sculpture. Heavy? It could take two burglars out with one fell swoop. Don't you love the way it's made from segments**, like armour plate, or perhaps chocolate orange**? An acquired taste perhaps.

- Armour plate works with the metal form of the sculpture (it is actually an orangutan, but it was exam pressure). But a chocolate orange – that says Christmas, doesn't it? (I hope you get one in your stocking).

Oh, you've noticed the television, have you? About four feet wide, I suppose. We chose it to fill the chimney breast and it **feels like a cinema** in the home. If you tuck your fingers under the sofa cushions you may be surprised by a stray piece of popcorn, unless Bunty and Leslie have found it of course. Yes, they are the poodles. I suppose they do look ridiculous: hard to believe they're descended from wolves. But they fit in with the other pageantry of curiosities. The two-foot tall St Nicholas, haunting the fireplace; the herd of elephants trooping the shelves. The carpet is a deep red, so deep it rarely gives up its secrets even to the hoover. The crud seems to work its way out of its fluffy folds **like splinters emerging from sore skin.**

- The fricative alliteration again suggests a sense of disgust.
- The simile matches this in disgusting subject matter, and the sibilance adds to this.

Have you seen the photographs? Borneo, that's the orangutan; Yellowstone, that's the buffalo looming out of the blizzard and the other one, the geyser, **steaming like a giant's sigh**. The gorilla with the babies takes pride of place because my wife is sentimental. I don't think she recognises herself in the image, though my son, perhaps, was the very spit of the one on the left.

- My wife is beautiful, and my son doesn't look like a gorilla. But it's funnier this way, and I am not writing as myself, but as a persona. (They won't read this anyway – it's just between you and me).

Time for a drink I think. Sink into the sofa and snug up to the cushions while I fetch the shortbread and Earl Grey. We just have time before the ankle-biters return from terrorising the garden with Bunty and Leslie, the barbarians at the gate.

- A sense of peace is created at the end, and this is emphasised by the sibilance of "Sink into the sofa and snug up to the cushions".

520 Words

What You Should Take From This

1. Notice how the creation of a persona allows you to come up with descriptions from their point of view.

2. In this case I have also chosen a persona with a slightly unpleasant personality who I also find quite funny. The reader doesn't have to - you are simply allowing the reader to picture his personality.

3. The other massive advantage of this is that I am not just describing the house, but through the voice of the persona, my reader also gets the extra benefit of picturing the grandfather. This means all my descriptions have layers to them, which will always be higher up the mark scheme.

Journey Through an Image

Journey Through a Painting in an Art Gallery

The following is based on a painting by Ralph Steadman. It is called 'A Load of Bankers'. You can Google it. Here is my version:

- The bankers are arranged in a clump, which is nearly a rectangle.
- They cram in on each other, and overlap, with hardly any space between each figure.
- They are all drawn in black ink, in cartoon style. Each face is emphasised. Every face appears aggressive, lips are turned down, or mouths are open as though to shout or bite.
- Each head is balding.
- For the most part, figures in the foreground are larger than those at the back. But the perspective is broken by a few figures who have large heads. At the centre, two of these are snarling at each other, and look like each wants to bit the other's neck.
- Behind these, are two faces, one on the left, the other on the right. They look bemused and out of place.
- Right at the back, and in the centre, stands a figure double the height he should be. He is in the centre of the painting's title, A Load of Bankers, which has been daubed in red paint just above the crush of bankers. Two splashes of red paint decorate the first A and B. If you peer closely, you'll notice small details of some faces which have been coloured in red.

Let's imagine you are asked to describe an image in the exam, but you don't want to. You want to describe 'A Load of Bankers'. How can you describe this image instead? You can place the first image, the one from the exam paper, in an art gallery. This is the image hanging next to it. Now, with the power of contrast, you can use the first image, to lead you to the one you prefer.

If you have no picture, you can probably relate this image to anything which comes up. Let's have some fun describing the image.

Task 1

- Make a list of 15 things you notice in the image. Write each one as a phrase or sentence.
- These will help you get the most out of the description when you read it.

Journey Through an Image Description

Starting with the second person - 'you' - is also a really good way of dragging the reader into the image with you.

What do you notice first? The writing **perhaps**: "a load of bankers". You scan the image for a sexual pun, but find nothing obvious. You notice red splodges of ink in mouths, and eyes, a mop of hair. Again, not sexual: more like blood.

Now you are lured in and you look for signs of violence. These **appear to be** verbal, with mouths set in square chins. Each mouth is a jagged line, whether open or shut, and those that are open display jagged teeth. Each face is uncomfortably close to its neighbour, **as though** fighting for territory, space, the other speaker's air.

Hands are mostly hidden, or behind backs, some curled up in a claw, **as though** revealing a predatory nature, a hidden threat. The figures are all men, none of them young. They are mostly uncompromisingly bald. You **wonder** if their ugliness has drawn them to banking, or if the occupation itself has stripped them of their hair.

The harshest faces are in the centre of the canvas, screaming at each other, **like caricatures of sharks**. Their mouths flail at each other. You look upwards, towards the one face which breaks above the scrum of bodies. He's a tall man who grimaces with a triumphant smile, but his eyes are blank, with no pupils. They are windows to an empty soul, the price of winning and rising to the top, **perhaps**.

This thought prompts you to look at the base of the scrum, or pyramid. You **decide** it is a hierarchy. The men at the base look beaten. Many have turned to look at you as they sink below the frame, cut off at eyes and noses, **as though** their mouths have been silenced.

It is a **puzzling** image. The men all **seem** to fixate on each other. They are not interested in you at all. You **wonder** how they earn their money, because the artist does not suggest they are exploiting the viewer. They desire much more to dominate each other. **Perhaps** it is a hopeful image, which imagines the whole banking system as a failure about to happen. At some point soon, the picture suggests, these men will turn on each other **like hyenas**, and tear each other apart. **Perhaps** the artist has gathered them here in the hope that it will happen now, so that more red ink can splatter the frame.

In the bottom left hand corner, the artist has signed his name, with the date, 2002. Even these numbers **look like eyes** between two ears, **as though history is watching**. You **wonder** if the artist saw the banking crisis of 2008 coming. You **worry** that one of the bankers looks like you.

449 Words

Others Things You Might Take From This Description

1. As always, verbs are most powerful. Pick 5 which you think are important here.
2. Contrast is king. Winners v losers, verbal violence v physical violence, hands v claws, man v animal, colour red v black and white, what we see and what the artist might intend us to think…
3. The circular structure, focusing on the change in 'you' at the end.
4. How each paragraph ends with a kind of question.
5. Ideas listed in threes.
6. How 'as though' works as a kind of simile.
7. How much of the description is simply describing what you actually see.
8. Deliberate repetition of words: **you, perhaps, as though, hidden, each**, give the writing a rhythm.
9. What soundscape did you notice? How does it match the mood of the scene?
10. Sometimes you can describe exactly what you see – treat the image as a painting in a gallery.

Journey Through a Photograph in an Art Gallery

IGCSE Question

On a long journey through an unfamiliar region, the bus on which you are travelling breaks down for a short time. Describe what you see and hear around you, and your thoughts and feelings as you wait.

Image from AQA question (my version of the actual photo – copyright issues!)

- Notice how the image from AQA would help you answer the IGCSE question, and that the IGCSE question could be answered with the AQA image.
- In other words, all description questions are the same - you can make them fit what you want to describe.

Describe a Photograph

Your eye is drawn to the figure on the jetty. You wonder why he's sitting with his back turned to the camera, as though in rebuke. **He's turned up his hood to gaze out at the lake**, possibly in defiance of the camera lens. **The jetty is empty**, and you imagine he sits, yearning for the boat to return, but whether for a long awaited return, or longed for escape, you do not know.

The lake must be deep, as the steep sided mountains reach down from the clouds and plunge beneath the icy waters. Yet the figure is wearing shorts, defying the weather, or challenging it to do its worst.

How long did the photographer wait before the bird perched on the post, and then swivelled to watch the sitter? **One eye observes us too, curious to see what you will do next.**

Your gaze looks at the surface, the gentle ripples and shadows slip in from the edges of the scene or, more alarming, from the depths. You notice a trail of light, leading from the jetty directly to the centre of the lake, where it widens like an open-armed invitation. You imagine the sitter ought to stand, to scan the light for clues, to see the spotlight as it promises to illuminate the star turn, a boat, a diver, a whale. But the star is going to make a late entrance, evidently. Nothing happens.

Who is photographing the scene, you wonder now? You imagine a parent, with a teenage son stroppily refusing to take part in whatever this is. The shorts suggest a cancelled walk around the shore, and the figure's thick waist implies a certain reluctance to exercise. And yet, the photographer must have insisted that they stay. Is it the spotlight he was waiting for, and nature herself the star? Her soft beauty radiates across the lake for the split second he has been waiting for.

Now the scene begins to make sense. A son, sulking on the shoreline he didn't want to visit anyway. The missing rucksack must mean he downed tools. And so his father has done the heavy lifting, with the camera and, we must suppose, a tripod.

God, the son must be thinking, staring at the incredible scene, when will this ever end?

377 Words

What You Should Take Away From This

- This has the same techniques as the writing about a painting, 'A Load of Bankers'.

- Can you remember what those techniques were?

- This is a short, concentrated piece, to show you that it is possible to get a grade 9 with fewer words.

- Introducing characters' viewpoints has allowed me to craft an ending from one character's point of view. I went straight for that writer's go-to technique – contrast. In this case a contrast with our expectations – I've spent the piece marvelling at the beauty of nature, only for the character to view it as a kind of tortured boredom.

Task:

1. Find an image and try this kind of writing for yourself.
2. Focus on 3 of the skills which you have seen in these two examples.
3. Use direct address: call the reader 'you'.

Answer Based on the AQA Paper 1 from June 2019

You don't have the picture here, but can find it at the AQA website.

However, just like the last description, I have simply described exactly what I see in the picture. So you will be able to picture it well, I hope.

I've also made a video about it for you: '2019 AQA Paper Grade 9 Description Answer Explained (Mr Salles).

The Market Place

The artist might have waited for just this moment. A man, a woman, a narrow path between stalls selling violence and carnage. The man looks predatory, his eyes in shadow and wearing what looks like a turtle neck jumper and a leather jacket. He blocks her path. The artist was probably a woman, because she sees her subject try to alter her path. She steps away from the swordfish, the parade of decapitated heads thrusting their blades into the air. But to her right hangs the flayed carcass of a pig, it's shiny muscles and sinews stripped of flesh and glistening. Perhaps this is the lesser of two evils. Behind the pig, a butcher sculpts its flank with a knife, like an artist. To her left the fish monger grabs hold of a fish-head's sword in a manner than can only be calculated to disgust her.

The scene looks French if the cheeses are anything to go by, and so we'll call the trapped woman trying to change direction Bernadette. Turtle-neck-leather man looks like a poser, the only person in the scene wearing more than shirt sleeves. He must love that jacket in this heat. We'll call him jacket man, Jacque for short.

Bernadette is not dressed to attract attention, not from the back anyway. Her waist looks like it is starting to thicken, though no one could call her fat. Coming up to middle age perhaps. The two small bags she's carrying might mean she lives alone, shopping for one, or the market may be a daily ritual. The artist hasn't cropped the scene too tightly. She wants us to revel in the colours, as well as the blood-red of meat. Bernadette has passed boxes of red peppers, crowding the scene with the blush of pink lobsters, and these jostle against the sheaths of green vegetables. Unlike the meat, they seem to lack a form or an identity. We can't tell if one box displays cauliflower or artichokes, and jammed next to it could be leeks or courgettes or even cobs of corn still in their green leaf sleeves.

So Jacque is drawn to the meat, and we wonder, is Bernadette just another kind of meat to him? Has he blocked the path to make her struggle to squeeze past him, for the thrill of it, exercising his power, telling himself perhaps that she would enjoy the forced contact as much as him? We are all animals after all, he might be thinking, standing among the carcasses.

Behind Jacque, and Bernadette can see this, three women are shopping. They might be a comfort to her, safety in numbers. But Jacque has passed them, and none of them have turned to glance at him. He might be harmless, after all. Their eyes are all downcast, focusing on the richness of the stalls, the competing aromas sending their hands into the purses, stroking coins, pondering which flavours to spend on. So perhaps Jacque is not a threat.

Perhaps it is she who has been waiting, waiting by the meat. Notice that her left arm is bent at the elbow, forearm in front of her. She makes as if to fend him off, but what of the fat pockets of his jacket? To brush past him in this narrow path must involve a collision, there is no way out of it now. The artist makes us wonder about the front of the dress. Jacque's eyes are also cast down at it. Cleavage. Meat. A suitable distraction.

Yes, that's it. She has waited for such a man. Her arm will meet him while his gaze is hypnotised. Her fingers will be quick, plucking his wallet from him with practiced ease.

623 Words

You have to bear in mind how much time you have in the exam. I could write this in 45 minutes. But what if I couldn't? I will improve as a writer if I edit it and reduce it to something I can write in the time limit. So here it is again in **469 words**.

The Market Place – Redrafted to Reduce Words

The artist might have waited for just this moment. A man, a woman, a narrow path between stalls **selling violence and carnage**. The man looks predatory, his eyes in shadow and wearing what looks like a turtle neck jumper and a leather jacket. He blocks her path. The artist was probably a woman, because she sees her subject try to alter her path.

She steps away from the swordfish, the **parade of decapitated heads** thrusting their blades into the air. But to her right hangs the flayed carcass of a pig, it's shiny muscles and sinews stripped of flesh and glistening. Perhaps this is the lesser of two evils.

Behind the pig, a butcher **sculpts its flank with a knife, like an artist**. To her left the fish monger grabs hold of a fish-head's sword in a manner than can only be calculated to disgust her.

The scene looks French if the cheeses are anything to go by, and so we'll call the trapped woman trying to change direction Bernadette. Turtle-neck-leather man looks like a poser, the only person in the scene wearing more than shirt sleeves. He must love that jacket in this heat. We'll call him jacket man, Jacque for short.

Bernadette is not dressed to attract attention, not from the back anyway. Her waist looks like it is starting to thicken, though no one could call her fat. Coming up to middle age perhaps. The artist wants us to revel in the colours, as well as the blood-red of meat. Boxes of red peppers crowding the scene with the blush of pink lobsters, and these jostle against the sheaths of green vegetables.

Jacque is drawn to the meat, and we wonder, is Bernadette **just another kind of meat** to him? Has he blocked the path to make her struggle to squeeze past him, for the thrill of it, exercising his power, telling himself perhaps that she would enjoy the forced contact as much as him? We are all animals after all, he might be thinking, standing among the carcasses.

Perhaps it is she who has been waiting, waiting by the meat. Notice that her left arm is bent at the elbow, forearm in front of her. She makes as if to fend him off, but what of the fat pockets of his jacket? To brush past him in this narrow path must involve a collision, there is no way out of it now. The artist makes us wonder about the front of the dress. Jacque's eyes are also cast down at it. Cleavage. **Meat**. A suitable distraction.

Yes, that's it. She has waited for such a man. Her arm will meet him while his gaze is hypnotised. Her fingers will be quick, plucking his wallet from him with practiced ease.

469 Words

Task:

1. Go back through it and see which bits were easy to get rid of. They are mostly extra things I had included from the character's point of view.
2. How many techniques have you been thinking about while working through the guide? Find examples of those in the above piece.

Journey Through Metaphor

A Student's Journey Taking an Exam

Let's imagine you are describing an exam. You could link all your imagery to a desert, or an explorer in the jungle. Linking your description around one key metaphor like this is a great way to show off. It also introduces what psychologists call a desirable difficulty – a difficulty which forces you to be creative.

The paper stretched out in front of her like a desert. Her eyes and fingers traced the questions and instructions like a map, leading the way to the promised oasis. Question one passed in the cool morning, before the sun could rise.

Question two gave her a boost, as though suddenly finding a camel to help on her journey. Next, question three presented a bigger challenge. She began to sweat, and noticed the first longings of thirst. She trod sand for a while, slipping, before she noticed the right path through the dunes.

Question four was uphill. Every step forward, her camel grew weaker. She scribbled furiously, desperate to find her way. Ahead, on the horizon, she was sure she saw it - the shimmering oasis of question 5. Head down, she placed one foot in front of the other, and hoped to make ground. After ten minutes, she looked up and panicked. The oasis had moved! Mirage, she thought. She shut her eyes, and prayed to the exam gods. She rummaged through the saddle bags of her revision, looking for the right answer. The camel eyed her mockingly, and began to spit.

Refusing to be distracted, she mounted up, dug her heels in and trotted towards question 5. This time, the oasis stayed on the horizon, and the palm trees grew larger with every passing minute.

227 Words, too short for an exam piece, but the grade 9 quality would still earn you a grade 7, even this short.

Task:
Work out how each description of the desert also fits the idea of the student taking the exam.

Writing Task:

1. Let's imagine you are describing a classroom. You could link all your imagery to a zoo.
2. Or write your own extended metaphor, comparing taking an exam to a different experience.
3. Or let's imagine you are describing a building site. You could describe all the machinery with imagery of dinosaurs.

A Toddler's Journey Through Metaphor, Exploring Space as an Astronaut

Let's imagine you are describing a child at play. You could link all your imagery to space exploration and an astronaut. All your similes and metaphors about play will refer to those two things.

The mother guides her daughter into the playpen, and sits on the edge to watch. The girl releases the adult fingers, and spacewalks towards the slide. In slow motion, she totters left and right, and then bounds towards the slide. She turns to look at her mother, to make sure the umbilical cord is still there, and then grips the hand rail. She clambers up, engaging her gravity boots, so she doesn't suddenly tip off into space.

Suddenly two boys arrive, screeching, and rushing up behind her. Are they going to be friendly aliens, wonders the mother? They get to the top of the ladder, where the girl sits at the lip of the slide, and she watches the boy's fingers flex with a life of their own. She knows he longs to push, and reaches towards her, ready to launch her off. But before he can, her daughter has already lifted off, and rockets downwards. She is propelled off the bottom lip, and crash lands on the soft matting.

"Again, mummy, again!" she yells.

175 Words

- Notice this isn't all an extended metaphor. It is a mix of several. At first the daughter is an astronaut on a spacewalk. But in the second paragraph she becomes a rocket.
- It is incredibly short, but even the harshest examiner couldn't give it less than a grade 5. I would give it a grade 6.

Task
1. Find the words which fit with space exploration and the toddler.

Writing Task
- Write your own description using space exploration compared to something else OR
- Write about astronauts in space and compare them to parents and toddlers.

Just Show me Methods for the Exam!

Weather Personification

- Here is a grade 7 description, based on bad weather
- This is grade 7 because the imagery is vivid, with great verbs which show us the violence of the weather.
- But it doesn't get a higher grade because the violence is not linked effectively - it would be better if it were all linked to wild animals, like the cat, or to the violence of the military.

Outside, the furious winds were stabbing anyone who walked through them – then disappearing, invisible. An army of clouds gathered in the sky, blocking out all sunlight and all hope, and casting an ominous shadow on the ground. The clouds were almost at bursting point: rain was imminent.

The storm began. The clouds began to hiss and spit like a savage cat, and the rain fell with the force of bullets. *It was as if the day itself was as angry as she was – and she was about to explode.*

Icy cold gusts of wind knocked the dark, grey, malevolent clouds across the sky. A weak, pale yellow sun struggled in vain to penetrate the bank of cloud; it was no use. The cold and the dark won that battle, hands down.

Task

- See if you can rewrite it so that all the imagery is linked.

Weather Personification 2

Here is a grade 9 description, based on bad weather

Winds flexed their muscles in the East, whipping the clouds into shape, marching them across the sky. The black jackboots of the rain tramped across the horizon, stamping cold onto the world beneath, as though some long dead tyrant had returned, armed with winter's fury.

The sky put on its black cape: the closest clouds armoured in battleship grey; those coming behind streaked with the black of coal smoke; those on the horizon dark as slate. Beneath a watcher might shut their eyes and pray for liberation, dreaming of the cavalry of sunlight.

(Yes, another extended metaphor for you to steal!)

Look at all the words which you can associate with battle or the army.

Task

Read through this description of the weather and make notes on how the imagery is made to link together with:

- The military
- The military of the past

How this Boosts Your Grade

It is full of ***simile, sibilance, powerful verbs, alliteration, contrast, interesting use of colour, a colon, complex sentences, accurate paragraphing, metaphor, powerful adjectives***.

That's 11 wow factors for the examiner.

If you memorise this structure and apply it in your exam, then your opening section will be at least a grade 7. Anyone can do this. Because the whole description is marked together, this alone will pull you up from a grade 4 to 5, or 5 to a 6, and very likely from a 6 to a 7.

The Kingsdown Method Checklist

Memorise the beginning of your description. Write your own metaphorical description of the weather – one for a positive experience, and one for a negative experience. These will fit any question in the exam.

At Kingsdown school, students practise using this checklist of 16 things to include in their writing. You can practice a few at a time, or all at once, depending on your skill levels. Once you can use them all, you will get at least a grade 7.

1. Start with the weather, using imagery you have memorised
2. Use a '**no, no, just' sentence**
3. Use a semi-colon or a colon in the weather description, to make sure you don't forget
4. The second paragraph starts with '**beneath the…sky, sat the…**' whatever you want to describe. This gives you a personification. You can change sat to a different verb *that a person would also do.*
5. Remember the colon introduces an explanation.
6. Uses contrast throughout.
7. Avoid animal imagery.
8. Use flashback from memories to provide contrast.
9. Lots of sibilance. Keep using words which begin with S.
10. List colour vocabulary like a Thesaurus – so instead of green: lime, sage, emerald, all in one sentence.
11. Have taste followed by an abstract noun – not something you can actually taste.
12. Sneak in a single, short sentence paragraph.
13. At the end, contrast with the weather you had at the beginning (that's where the character's memory easily comes in).
14. Then, in the final paragraph, have a final couple of lines which bring you back to the present.
15. End the final paragraph with short sentences.
16. Consciously craft your writing, rather than write loads.

These are useful to you if you are aiming to improve your grade to a 5, 6 or 7.

Kingsdown Exam Method – Model Answer

Description of The Beach

The sun dripped warmth like hot wax, both soothing and smarting the bathers below. The beach glowed with light, the heat so strong it dazzled, **and a thousand sunglasses took in the view**. The horizon rippled, like a bronze shield beaten by a hammer, as though some Greek God had been reborn to hurl shafts of glorious light on the grateful **sun worshipers** below.

The sky showed off its artist's trickery: cobalt blue depths, azure outlines to the few white clouds, a sapphire halo around the sun. Beneath, **the sun bathers shut their eyes and sun still glowed behind the blackness of their lids, yellow fire, sparking and fading**. The sea stretched out in lazy ripples, in a reflection of the perfect sky.

Beneath the soothing sky, cliffs cradled the edges of the beach, like powerful arms protecting against the wind, so that the white topped waves broke themselves against their rocky elbows, hidden from view. *No wind whipped the sand towards oiled bodies, no ice-creams were peppered with sandy grit; just a gentle breeze soothed the skin*.

Young men and women bronzed themselves, preening and strutting, exotic birds displaying themselves to each other. The women splashing in the water with exaggerated screams; reclining seductively in beach chairs, glancing provocatively beneath the brims of their sun hats; turning on their fronts with bikini bottoms scribbled on their behinds like exclamation marks.

Whatever the men did, they did loudly: shouting encouragement through ball games; laughing delightedly as the missed balls landed nearer the languid women; striking poses with beer bottles, back slappings and iron pumped physiques.

Families played their own games. Children charged the shallows, while fathers followed, and mothers clutched their books, for once transported to a different paradise, where the romance, tragedy and passion were safe, unreal, trapped tamely on their pages.

Nothing could go wrong here.

One grandfather stood alone, staring out to sea, imagining the horizon. It would have been night time, the sea alive with a slick, black skin of spilt oil, burning with fury. He could taste the sailors' fear as though it was his own. They must have jumped from the torpedoed battleship, desperate not to surface, fighting for air, through the burning carpet of the sea. How his father had struggled to breathe, so close to the shore. Only half his face had been sacrificed, but he had gained a life. Life, his father had said, life worth living.

Later the sky looked down with a softer heat, the sands became kinder to the tender soles of feet, like embers in a dead fire. Children were coaxed from the murmuring sea. The sun lost its bronze glow. Sandcastles melted. Responsibilities faded. Thoughts turned to love.

453 Words

Did you spot the sentences in italics?

Task

Go back to the Kingsdown Rules and highlight this passage to find each one.

Kingsdown Method 2

There is also a method for *structuring* your description. It looks like this:

1. **Weather** - to set your tone (and you can memorise it in advance)

2. **Zoom Out** - to get a wide-angle perspective

3. **Zoom In** - to focus on detail

4. **Zoom In** - to focus on detail

5. **Zoom In** - to focus on detail

6. **Zoom Out** - to create a contrast (which can easily be done by returning to the weather, showing a change).

This gives your writing 6 paragraphs. I've 'cheated' below by adding a 3 word paragraph.

Model Answer

Weather

The sun dripped warmth like hot wax, both soothing and smarting the **early shoppers striding out** below. The land glowed with light, the heat so strong it dazzled. The horizon rippled, like a bronze shield beaten by a hammer, as though some Greek God had been reborn to hurl shafts of glorious light on the grateful **commuters** below, **strolling the cobbled streets on the way to work**.

Zoom Out

The sky showed off its artist's trickery: cobalt blue depths, azure outlines to the few white clouds, a sapphire halo around the sun. Beneath, a watcher might shut their eyes and **listen to the pigeons, their cooing** stretched out in lazy ripples, **as they fed for scraps on pavements, indifferent** to the perfect sky.

Zoom In

Beneath the golden sky sat an old man, the pigeons surrounding him a daily ritual. His bag perched at his side, ready to spill a hundred seeds to his feathered companions. How soft their feathers looked. Sometimes they let him stroke them, staring up at him with their red, evil eyes. Yes, he saw these little dinosaurs for what they were, tamed killers, with beaks as sharp as nails. But he loved them. They needed him. That was rare these days.

Zoom In

He sat with his usual armour: an umbrella, furled tightly **like a lance**, ready **to joust** a dragon should one venture up the cobbled streets; his **helmet** stereotypically French, a flat cap, light to ward off the sun, as worn by the Tour de France riders for a century. ***No more cycling for him snaking through mountain passes; no more ciders pressed into his hands by country barmaids welcoming*** a knight ***on two wheels, just these birds, the feathered kinds***. This one cooed as he stroked it.

Warm, like youth.

Zoom In

In sunlight he could taste his youth again. The rays unzipped him, and he could imagine stepping out of his old skin like a wrinkled suit, to reveal the heaving **breastplate** of his chest, ready for the mountains, ready for all the hairpins life had thrown at him, the glorious peak of his wife (Mon Dieu how he missed her) and the breakneck descents of cancer and old age. Youth flooded back to him each morning. Until he tried to stand.

Zoom Out - weather, the past, the future

The sun's wax now seemed to cool. He turned his eyes from the red and black flag flapping next to him, a terrible reminder of the past, he thought, like a swastika. The umbrella stood beside him, preparing for the worst. He clasped his hands together in silent prayer. He shut his eyes against the coming day.

430 Words

(There's that extended metaphor again, with the old man portrayed as a knight. That's why the examiner is desperate to give me a grade 9).

Task

- Go through the Kingsdown Method - the 16 things to include in your description.
- Highlight an example of each in the description above.

Six Cameras Method

The **six cameras** technique always works, whatever your subject. It works whether you are writing an exam answer, or taking your time writing a story for pleasure or for publication.

It works best when the action takes place over a short amount of time.

Six Cameras is a good name. SixCam if you want to sound trendy. ZMZMZM if you want a weird brand name.

This is it:

1. **Zoom** Out – flock of geese
2. Motif – symbol or image – guitar
3. **Zoom** in – face stewardess
4. Motif – music
5. **Zoom** out - space eyed view, God
6. Motif - guitar

On the left is the structure. On the right is what I jotted down in front of my class.

A **motif** is just an image you or object your keep coming back to. In the Kingsdown method it is simply called a **Zoom In**.

The picture we were looking at was of a mother and young son, looking out at a runway with a plane on it. I asked my students to write down anything that came to mind. My class, being teenagers, mainly wrote about plane crashes.

"Write about a plane crash sir."

Left to their own devices, 50% of teenagers will probably kill something when they write creatively. That's how entertainment works these days – guns, explosions, zombies, terrorism, computer games with mega-slaughter…

So the rule is nobody dies.

Now, take your six cameras and place them around the scene. The cameras gave me the list on the right. I just wrote down the first thing for each that came into my head. That's it. That's your whole plan.

Now all I had to do was crash my plane, but not describe anybody dying.

Easy.

Model Answer: Wings

Zoom Out – flock of geese

The V followed its normal trajectory, the lead swapping as though by telepathy, in a strange choreography which had developed over millions of years without planes. Perhaps why the lead bird did not notice the Airbus, rising towards it. Perhaps that is why the flock followed blindly, faithful to the goose in front, as the engines rose to meet them like a greeting on a warm summer's day.

Motif – symbol or image – guitar

At the window, Lisa sat, cradling her new guitar. She was eight years old, and going to Nashville, to join her father at last. He had given her this red guitar as a present, and a promise that he would teach her to play like an angel. Her eyes turned to the window, registering the silent disaster as the birds met the engine on her left-hand side. Something was wrong with this picture, and she thought she heard the guitar begin to play.

Zoom In – face stewardess

The stewardess with the blond hair, and the tired eyes, fed up of passengers asking her question after question, trip after trip, felt it first, as though she were a Jedi knight feeling a disruption in The Force. She smiled, realising that her boyfriend would be surprised at the Star Wars reference. But something was wrong. This wasn't turbulence. There was a disruption in the Force.

Motif – music

In slow motion, the theme tune played. Dum dum dum, dum – de - dum. An image of black boots and a black helmet appeared. Instantly, she knew the symbol for what it was. She suddenly realised why he was called Darth, a short syllable away from total blackness, eternal blackness, the coming blackness.

Bart was playing on his phone again. At sixteen he knew better than to have the volume turned up, so that the middle-aged couple next to him could hear his appalling music leaking out of his ears, in a slow trickle that had built up to a flood, drowning them both in unexpressed anger as the flight wore on. How the music had droned. The wife saw the geese first, and some part of her brain, the reptilian part she knew, suddenly kicked in. Anger rose in her like fire, no like petrol thrown on to a fire, and flames of rage, huge and overwhelming strobed the back of her skull. She turned to the boy, placed one hand on his earphones, and prepared for what she knew was coming.

He looked into her eyes, and watched her lips move: "we don't need no education, we don't need no…" But he would never know what she didn't need.

Zoom Out - space eyed view, God

Who was it who gazed down silently at the scene? The pilot looked up, as though in prayer. He had felt it too, and knew the procedure, the checklist that he and his co-pilot would jump into, the years of training kicking in. But he feared this would not be enough. He looked up, hoping for a sign.

Only the clouds gazed back at him. Lisa noticed them too. Fluffy, like a child's drawing. Unreal. But they looked down with indifference.

In seconds the entire flock was gone. The engines roared with flame, and triumph or rage, it was impossible to tell. The clouds looked on sightlessly, without care.

Motif

The stewardess turned toward the flash of red. Lisa had lifted her guitar, and was taking it out of the case for the very first time.

564 Words

What to learn from this description:

1. The 6 changes of camera angle always work, because they give you different perspectives.
2. Because each camera is filming action which is happening over the same 60 seconds, you won't end up writing a story. (Although, the brilliant structure 6 Cam gives you, with the motif, means that you will always be able to submit it as a story if you wish).
3. Because the cameras are filming within the same sixty seconds (or even shorter), they easily build up to a climax, which is the ending. You don't have to plan it in advance.
4. Start with a contrast, as this automatically presents a crisis or conflict. The whole camera structure makes sure that each shot is a contrast to the last.
5. Camera angles allow you to think in moving pictures, which make it easier to think of similes and metaphors.
6. Give your character's backstory quickly, so we know their thoughts and some history.
7. **Try to start each sentence with a different word.**
8. **Slow down time with adverbs – notice they appear in my 'slow motion' paragraph.**
9. Enjoy writing, using allusions. You should spot The Simpsons, Star Wars, Pink Floyd.
10. Have a circular ending, referring back to the motif you started with.
11. Twist the reader's expectations at the end. It is more tragic if the girl has never played her guitar before.
12. End it just before the death. Let the reader add up two plus two.
13. Having a motif will always give your story structure. In the days when every newspaper published short stories, a writer who got stuck might follow this advice, "just introduce a man with a gun." But, as we know, we are trying not to kill anyone! Our equivalent is the motif. It gives your story structure, and as you keep going back to it, it will give you a focus for your ending.

(Bold means these count double, as they are also in the 16 marks available for AO6 Technical Accuracy).

So what do you know?

At this stage in the course, you ought to be thinking like a writer. This means asking yourself these questions:

1. What am I learning about really good metaphors and similes?
2. Is the imagery linked together, or is there any I would change to make a better link?
3. Is there an extended metaphor? If not, could I put one in?
4. Which bits of contrast work really well?
5. Are there any verbs which stand out?
6. How do the allusions to songs work, and to Star Wars? Could I do something similar in my writing?
7. What do I notice about the harsh sounds and consonance?
8. What do I notice about the soft sounds and sibilance?
9. Do I understand the idea of a motif, and could I use it?
10. Why are there always 10 things in a list - oooh, that reminds me, do the sentences have any interesting ways of listing that I could steal?

And so on….

Writing Task

1. Write a description based on this photograph (250-500 words)
2. Imagine it is an image in an art gallery, and you are going to:
    - Describe what you see
    - Enter into the mind of the character
    - Enter into the thoughts and relationship with the photographer
    - If you like, end each paragraph with a kind of question
    - Use similes

Yasmine's Work

(A grade 9 student stuck on grade 6/7 writing)

Yasmine's mother emailed me during one of the Covid lockdowns. I don't normally do any tutoring, but you know, everyone was stuck at home.

Yasmine was an academic student, but wasn't getting top grades in English. She was doing *everything* her teacher told her to do, but it still didn't seem to make any difference. Her problems were very typical. They all have to do with how we teach descriptions in schools.

We say: "use loads and loads of descriptive techniques and adventurous vocabulary", which is a bit like saying, "chuck all your favourite foods into one recipe". Each is delightful on its own, but mixed together just makes no sense. It would probably make you sick.

This is how she used to write before the advice I gave her and am about to give you:

On that Sunday afternoon, Farmelius strode down **the perpetual field that stretched across the landscape.** Patches of **dove-white** clouds swept **in silence across** the **azure** sky on a clear spring day. A cool breeze **softened the sultry air, whilst the golden sphere in the corner illuminated the** blunt mountains that stood with substantial pride. There was a pungent smell of nature that infused the atmosphere. **Water sprinkled from above just 45 minutes ago,** soaking the soil, but the tremendous light and heat had sucked it dry. **Farmelius did it. He became the wealthiest farmer with the most fruitful land in the world – something his father had failed to do.**

'I wish you were here,' said Farmelius while his voice cracked, and eyes sparkled.

He continued to plod down the rows of fruits and vegetables, **like lines on a piece of paper.** He looked at the dry soil **with a hefty crimson digging fork that rested on his left shoulder. Its fingers lay on top of his straw sunhat, as if to comfort him.** The mud on his grey leather boots had dried up and began to break apart, slowly falling away as he travelled. **His trousers were grey and crinkled and had 4 bright patches where the dye had faded away.** His fingers naturally curled towards his body as he looked down to find a shimmering object. It was a golden ring – one he had seen before. He picked it up. Farmelius remembered a time when he and his father were running around the field whilst **water poured down from the sombre sky, like a broken tap that could not be fixed.** It was so powerful that upon returning to shelter his father's ring was gone, despite his huge hands. The water trickled down his father's beard and dropped on Farmelius' head, **as if it was not already drenched.**

Farmelius slid his index finger through the ring and stretched his arm out, slightly tilting it in the sun's rays.

It was divine.

On that Sunday afternoon, Farmelius gazed at the field, at the row of red roses to his right that had blossomed early. **The golden sphere started to fade;** it was nearing the end of a Sunday afternoon.

What do You Notice?

- It's really very good, because it does exactly what she has been taught to do – chuck in as much description as you can.
- Yasmine uses heaps of descriptive techniques.
- She has very sophisticated vocabulary.
- She has zoomed in on detail.
- She's used a range of ambitious choices of colour.
- There are adjectives a-plenty.

You get the idea. So why couldn't she get top grades?

Check out the phrases in bold. These are pieces of description that don't really help the reader. They are just there to show that she is describing.

By 'help the reader' I mean help the reader picture the scene and understand the character's feelings. Everything else gets in the way.

The easiest way to think about this is to act on the one piece of advice I gave Yasmine:

Think of a book you really enjoy. Write a description that would fit into that book.

This is what Yasmine wrote next:

The book I am inspired by is **"The Star of Kazan"** by Eva Ibbotson

Pine woods

Hot sunshine streamed down through the canopy of pines. Green and yellow sunlight, distorted, like a vintage photograph, turned dust to gold. Golden specks floated to earth. I wolfed down deep lung fulls of the hot pine scent and mulch. I padded across the carpet of needles and paused. Outside the grove, shadows lay in wait. They swallowed the light and laughed, silently, at the innocent visitors to the wood. They sulked at my bliss and their gaping mouths grew wider.

Unheeded by darkness or light, a red squirrel nonchalantly jumped from branch to branch. Its feathered tail twitched and it leaped over the divide of shadows and sun rays. Needles fell under its minuscule paws. As it grew closer, I noted the russet tufts on its ears. Cautiously, haloed by the light, it lifted its tiny nose and sniffed the air. I laughed at how humane its gestures were. It bounded away, frightened by the sudden sound, left me to raven croaks and the whistling of the breeze in the pines.

Things I would like improve on in my writing (in order of priority):

1. Clear simple writing with occasional "flashy" vocabulary to good effect
2. How to make my writing flow (I feel it's too stilted at the moment)
3. How to use the mental "creator" rather than the mental "editor" and not mix the two up!
4. How to create memorable imagery

5. An effective use of contrasts

6. How to plan effectively (for description)

Notice how Yasmine isn't asking for me to assess her work. I never gave her a grade. She has just decided on targets she would set herself. They are not based on a list of techniques I have given her. They are based on what she has noticed about the descriptions in the books she likes.

She pretty much stopped needing my help right there!

The next task I set Yasmine was to still write in the same way, but to start each sentence with a new word.

Misty vapour cascades down the waterfall. Roaring and tumbling, the girl gazes awestruck as it pounds the rocks in the pool below. It has no mercy. Square, sculpted rocks that resemble abstract architecture, frame the water exhibit.

Dappled sunlight filters through the patchwork tree tops. Cropped turf rings the edge of the pool. She lowers a toe into the water. And instantly regrets it. Arctic in temperature, the cold shoots into her feet, her calves, her thighs. Gasping, she draws it back.

Twisted, gnarled, thick tree trunks are the custodians of this sacred space. They lean precariously over the waterfall, inserted in between the crevices. Birches crowd the grove; their slim, silvery elegance contrasts the older trees.

Droplets of water vapour catch in her ginger curls. Roars echo off the stone, as hymns echo off cathedral walls. She closes her eyes and relishes the sound.

Above, an aeroplane cuts into the seamless blue sky, engine grumbling loudly. It jars the ethereal atmosphere, and the girl opens her eyes.

Buzzards wheel and circle on the thermals. Winds carry them higher into the heavens.

Below, the girl takes the plunge. She slides off the grassy bank and into the pool. Taking a deep breath, she pinches her nose and dives.

(208 Words)

Notice that this writing does not show off that it is descriptive. It is simply description that you could find in a fiction book.

Some brilliant features of this writing:

1. Each sentence starts with a different word.

2. Hardly an adverb, and they are used to slow down time.

3. Careful attention when selecting exactly the right verb.

4. Yasmine is a writer who listens to the sounds words make – making use of soft sounds and sibilance, with harsh sounds where these fit the change of mood.

5. The present tense forces us into the scene.

6. Adjectives are often listed to build layers of description.

7. Sentences built around a rhythm, in lists.

8. She uses metaphor more than simile, which is more engaging.

9. The description is told in images, like photographs or 5 second snatches of video.

10. Deliberate use of contrast creates drama (even when nothing much happens).

Yasmine tries the same techniques again, starting each sentence with a different word:

Fog starts to shroud the valley. Rocks jut from the mountain's vertical drop.

To the left, a stone circle lies at the foothills. Clumps of moss cling to their statuesque silhouettes. They throw faint shadows onto the boggy terrain, and birds hurry to their roosts.

Right of the peak, waterfalls drop down other mountain tops. White water against black rock. Wriggling from their birthplace, they tumble away, eager to leave the solemn summits.

Scotland lies like a map in front of him. Every dip, every mound, every miniature mark on the horizon is memorised. To say he loves this place would be a gross understatement. Sheep droppings litter the turf randomly; the only clue civilisation still dwells below. But for an occasional raven, this peak is empty. His for reflection, one last time. Wind nips his fingers. They are already numb, already red and sore, but he barely notices.

Darkness surrounds the villages underneath him. Fearful of the unknown blackness, people light oil lanterns. Fog draws his cloak tighter.

Cracks in the bushes behind alert him. Deer? And in front, gliding down from the fading sky, a single white feather floats to the precipice. Pushed by a merciless gust of wind, the feather descends once again. Above it, the boy turns his back and returns down the slope into the unknown black called night.

What to notice about this technique:

- It forces you to be inventive, and this creates interesting writing

- A lot of the vocabulary is inspired by texts you know – you can feel Macbeth in this piece, with the reference to 'roosts', and the bird is a 'raven'. Perhaps we feel Exposure by Wilfred Owen possibly gives us the description of the merciless wind.

- Creating a persona, who is in the scene, but who is not doing lots of things, creates interesting perspectives.

- Focusing on individual words makes you pay attention to the sound of words – look at the alliteration and sibilance in this piece.

There is only one change I would make, which would be to delete the last three words. We can infer them from what has gone before.

Apart from that, though, Yasmine's last two pieces really could fit into a real book, published by one of her favourite authors.

Here she does the same describing a hawk. This time I didn't just ask her to start each sentence with a new word. Instead, she also had to start using the random 15 sentence technique I taught you earlier in my memory of learning to ride a motorbike:

1. Slicing the air with her wings, the hawk swoops down.
2. Gracefully landing, she has the air of aristocratic indifference.
3. Piercing eyes darting around, suspicious of the plain, good-natured, plebeian, sparrows, she ruffles her shoulders and grips the branch tighter with her wrinkled, yellow talons.
4. The drab house sparrows could not begin to compare to the hawk, bless them. They know it and fly away, so as not to be compared unfavourably against her.
5. Although the hawk reigns supreme over the lesser birds, she is disliked.
6. Humans do not want her.
7. Why? She chases the newborn fledglings like a spaniel after rabbits. For fun, to watch the fear grow in their round eyes as she approaches.
8. Perhaps it is mean, she thinks.
9. But she keeps herself to herself. It is lonesome at times, for the others fear her. You can see the loneliness in her eyes.
10. Because a hawk never shows that she cries, she bites the other birds with her contemptuous looks. Her eyes are slits of unquenched fire.
11. Light scintillates off her shining wings. Should she lose her cruel arrogance, she would be beautiful.
12. Epitomising elegance, she lifts off into the subdued, grey sky.
13. Sunlight cloaks her lustrous silhouette.
14. Why is it that hawks are, unquestionably, the royalty of the avian kingdom? Is it their inborn belief that they are superior?
15. Whatever it is, when a hawk flies, one is instinctively compelled to look at it. For a hawk is no countess; nor a lady, nor a duchess. A hawk is undoubtably a queen.

Amazing, isn't it?

Try it for yourself – it really works.

Printed in Great Britain
by Amazon